A NATION TOO GOOD TO LOSE

Renewing the Purpose of Canada

The Right Honourable Joe Clark

KEY PORTER·BOOKS

This book is dedicated to all those Canadians who love their country, and are prepared to help it flourish.

Canadian Cataloguing in Publication Data

Clark, Joe, 1939-
A nation too good to lose : renewing the
purpose of Canada

ISBN 1-55013-603-8

1. Canada – Politics and government – 1993-   2. Nationalism – Canada.   3. Federal government – Canada.   I. Title

FC98.C53 1994   320.971   C94-900731-5
F1034.2.C53 1994

The publisher gratefully acknowledges the assistance of the Canada Council, the Ontario Publishing Centre and the Government of Ontario.

Key Porter Books Limited
70 The Esplanade
Toronto, Ontario
Canada M5E 1R2

Printed and bound in Canada

94 95 96 97 98 5 4 3 2 1

CONTENTS

ACKNOWLEDGEMENTS

LITERALLY THOUSANDS OF PEOPLE HAVE HELPED ME WRITE THIS book, from citizens whose frankness jolted me free of old assumptions, to constitutional experts and negotiators, to foreigners who often see Canada's advantages more clearly than we do.

I am particularly grateful to several friends, who had worked with me in the past, and came to my aid again as this was being written, and to Beverly Endersby, who edited the final text.

Naturally, the two people who helped me most are Maureen and Catherine, who shared so many of my experiences of our country, and were usually willing to offer advice.

ONE

THE
"BETTER WAY"

FIFTEEN YEARS AGO THIS SPRING, I LED TO OFFICE WHAT QUEBEC journalists enjoy calling "le gouvernement éphémère de Joe Clark." On May 22, 1979, my party won a majority of seats in every province except three – New Brunswick, Quebec, and Newfoundland – and then, in December, we were defeated on a budget vote in Parliament. That led to another election, in February 1980, and Pierre Elliott Trudeau returned to office.

There is a tradition that the portraits of former prime ministers hang in the corridors of Parliament. With what struck me as unseemly haste, portrait artists began to ask me to consider their services. There is a finality to being hung in Parliament, and I hope to delay that fate as long as I can. While my life as a political candidate is behind me now, there are other interesting things I want to do before being locked in a frame. I take the same attitude towards memoirs, and this short book is not intended as either recollection or history, but as a reflection on issues that run deep in Canada and on which my views may help other Canadians come to decisions about their country.

I am, by nature, an optimist. That sustained me through a turbulent political career and, particularly, during the negotiations and referendum on the Charlottetown Accord. When others had declared those negotiations deadlocked, and believed there was no hope of getting an overall agreement, I literally made people stay at the table. I was the chairman of the process, and it was difficult for others to declare a failure if I would not. The proverbial test of optimism is whether you believe the glass is half empty or half full. All of my instincts are to treat the slightest amount of moisture as proof that the Canadian glass is filling – that things are getting better, not worse.

So I have been surprised by my own pessimism since the defeat of the accord in the referendum. For a while, I attributed that to physical exhaustion, or the undeniable fact that I was too close to the process – how could I not take personally the rejection of an agreement I had spent months negotiating? I stepped away from the consuming life of politics, and wanted to be someplace where the daily news would not be about things I used to do. Maureen, Catherine, and I spent the year at the University of California at Berkeley, near San Francisco, where there is scant danger of hearing about Canada. Apart from reports of bad weather moving down from the north, the only references made to Canada were when the Blue Jays became champions of the American game and, briefly and feverishly, when the San Jose Sharks challenged the Maple Leafs.

Active political life – probably any active life – leaves virtually no time to reflect on what you are seeing or doing. Events crowd into other events. You react to crisis and surprise and opportunity, and rarely have time to ask yourself, or discuss with your friends and associates, where all those actions are leading, what they mean.

I had spent nearly seven years as secretary of state for External Affairs. That is a wonderful portfolio but, by its nature, it takes you away from day-to-day developments at home. It turned out, after I was asked to lead the constitutional discussions, that it helped to have been away. For one thing, I was not caught up so directly in the traumas of the Meech Lake Accord. But, more important, I had to immerse myself in my country again, and I realized how much it had changed and how unsettled it had become. There was stark evidence that established practices weren't working any more. The tradition of having premiers and the prime minister decide questions in closed meetings — so-called executive federalism — had broken down with the Meech Lake Accord. The tradition of public hearings led by a committee of Parliament had lost credibility during the next round of constitutional discussions. Generally, there was an anger, a distemper, in the country.

I have always tried to listen carefully, to understand what people are really telling me. As I listened to literally thousands of Canadians during the eighteen months between my appointment and the referendum, my sense grew that the changes in Canada were far deeper than our traditional systems or assumptions could comprehend.

The simple fact that we needed constitutional negotiations at all indicated that the Canadian system was not working as well as it needed to. The most urgent case was in Quebec, and it is important to bear in mind the background to attitudes in that province. "Sovereignty-association" had been defeated in the referendum of 1980 in part because then prime minister Pierre

Trudeau had promised, in a powerful speech in Paul Sauvé Arena on May 14, 1980, that there would be a renewal of the Canadian federation. That was a persuasive performance, just six days before Quebec voted; yet the promise that Quebecers heard was not kept. The issue, for most Quebecers, related to the powers their province would exercise in Confederation, but that was not what the Trudeau government had in mind. Instead, in November 1981, Mr. Trudeau and the nine premiers of English-speaking Canada made a different kind of constitutional deal. That was the decision to bring the constitution home from Britain, introduce a charter of rights, and change the constitutional amending formula. To make matters worse, they made that deal in the absence of Quebec premier René Lévesque. Whatever the merits of those changes, they were not seen in Quebec as keeping the promise made in Paul Sauvé Arena. The unhappiness in the province was made worse by the fact that the deal had been cut without the agreement of the premier of Quebec, and then given effect despite the unanimous opposition of the National Assembly of that province.

I was leader of the official opposition in the House of Commons during that period and was very active in the debate, including in Quebec. That experience led me to believe that those events had generated a sense of betrayal in Quebec that, unless reversed, would drive Quebec to separation. The Meech Lake Accord sought to solve that problem, but, in doing so, it triggered a barrage of opposition from other groups who, in turn, felt left out of that process.

It has been suggested that, since the Meech Lake Accord failed, its goals should never have been pursued. That is an odd attitude in a country where progress has always depended upon taking reasonable risks, and it reveals an unusually timid interpretation of the responsibility of government. It assumes that Canada could simply have ignored the accelerating alienation of Quebec, whose *de facto* withdrawal from federal-provincial meetings had already set us on the path to becoming a nine-province country.

The Trudeau government, which had excluded Quebec from the process of constitutional change in 1982, had neither the will nor the authority to repair that damage. However, the election, in 1984, of a new majority government, led by Brian Mulroney, presented a fresh opportunity, not least because the new prime minister had won strong support in Quebec. I may be a prejudiced witness, but one reading of recent Canadian history is that Liberal prime ministers can inherit their support in Quebec, but Progressive Conservative prime ministers have to earn it. Prime Minister Mulroney's personal authority was matched by the unanimous determination of the provinces to try to bring Quebec back into the constitutional family, and so, at the annual Premiers' Conference in Edmonton, the provinces began the process that led to the Meech Lake Accord.

In my view, the opposition that mushroomed at the end of that process was not particularly anti-Quebec, nor even directed at the principles of the Meech Lake Accord. Instead, just as the 1982 agreement had become a symbol of the exclusion of Quebecers, the Meech Lake Accord became a symbol of the exclusion of other Canadians – aboriginals, Northerners, women, proponents of Senate reform, and a public who turned against the tradition of closed-door executive federalism.

Exclusion is always an issue in a democracy. But it matters more when you think that those interests you hold as most important will suffer as a consequence. The reactions to exclusion expressed during the Meech Lake process were not just populist distemper; they were more focused. Just as Quebec believed its real interests were at risk in 1982, so, at Meech, did aboriginals, some Western Canadians, and other groups. And when the system didn't respond, they stepped away from it. Quebec stopped coming to federal-provincial meetings; aboriginals didn't accept the legitimacy of decisions made at Meech Lake; and public opinion in English Canada swelled to oppose those decisions.

I think more Canadians than we realize have stepped away from the assumptions that used to prevail in Canada. Yet our systems and the actions of our leaders are still based on those familiar assumptions. As a consequence, it would seem that many Canadians don't define their country as their leaders do, and don't treat the Canadian system as legitimate. If that is so, the need is urgent for Canadians to consider what that means for our future, and whether, and how, we can achieve a consensus that fits the modern Canada.

One factor in particular distinguishes our present situation. In the past, "national unity" was code for troubles in the relations between Quebec and "the rest of the country." The conventional wisdom was that, if we could settle the "Quebec problem," everything else would fall into place. That "wisdom" was reflected perfectly in the decision, leading to the Meech Lake Accord, to consider the issues in two stages: first, the "Quebec Round"; then, the rest. That two-part process didn't work. The Meech Lake experience proved clearly that those concerned with issues other than Quebec will not take second place. They consider their causes to be as important as those of Quebecers, and they won widespread support for that view in public opinion outside Quebec. A gap developed between the people who had been immersed in constitutional discussions, who defined the issues in traditional ways, and the public, for whom that conventional wisdom had broken down. In my judgement, that shift is permanent. "National unity" now means more than keeping Quebec in Canada.

Yet conventional wisdom dies hard. Many Canadians still believe that, if we could rebuff separatism one more time, we would put our problems behind us. I ran up against that attitude regularly in official Ottawa, and still find it among many Canadians who think and care about constitutional issues. It is a comforting illusion, because it pretends we will not have to contemplate many real changes in our country.

I think that conventional wisdom misjudges Quebec, because it underestimates the durability of Quebec's requirement for changes, whether it remains a part of Canada or not. And it misjudges both the intensity of the vocal demand for changes outside Quebec and the quiet growth of the sense that the Canada of traditional assumptions may not be worth keeping. As I argue later, that larger malaise seems to me to be the fundamental issue facing Canada.

It is probably understandable that, among Quebecers, the overwhelming preoccupation with their own agenda led to the assumption that aboriginal and Western issues are, at best, secondary and, at worst, a diversion. But that self-absorption is seen as indifference, or hostility, by the rest of the country, which itself constitutes a significant obstacle to a renewal of Canada as a whole nation.

In fact, Quebec has not shown much fraternal interest in the rest of the country. An exception was Claude Ryan, who, as editor of *Le Devoir*, made regular pilgrimages to other parts of Canada. I remember meeting him in Edmonton in the early 1960s, when I was editing the student newspaper, *The Gateway*, at the University of Alberta. He was an impressive figure, but, in retrospect, what was most remarkable was the simple fact that he bothered to come, that he sought out Canadians in other provinces, not just to tell us about Quebec but, in our case, to ask about Alberta, to talk about Canada. That has not happened very often, at least in the relation between Quebec and Western Canada. During the several years in which I urged Albertans to accept the Official Languages Act, or the legitimacy of the "distinct society" of Quebec, there were not many Quebecers who asked about the history or the culture or the aspirations of Alberta.

In any event, Canada's troubles today go well beyond those issues traditionally described as constitutional. Today's troubles are expressed in various ways: as apocalyptic warnings about the national debt, antagonism towards immigrants, anger at "young offenders" and "welfare cheats," a conviction that we are not keeping pace with our competitors, or a hundred other particular complaints. There is nothing uniquely Canadian about any of those issues – except that we may lack the will to resolve them. When similar anxieties arise in other Western nations, those societies respond from a common ground of certainty about their own purpose and future. Do Canadians have that common ground? When we confront the pressures that assault all modern societies, can we assume a common purpose or a common future? Or have both become quiet casualties of the divisions and indifference in Canada?

I believe that is what is happening now and that it could get more serious. My fear is that, left to our own devices, our own divisions, Canadians could drift farther apart, lamenting the gradual loss of Canada, but not doing anything practical to stop it.

Not everything breaks with a bang. Sometimes things just come apart, undone by little incidents that get out of hand. For example, I was startled, this Stanley Cup spring, by how easily and angrily some Vancouver hockey fans interpreted the early starting time of a Canucks-Leafs game as proof of a deep-seated anti-B.C. bias in the country. Of course time zones are irritating, and Western Canadians have had to accommodate the Central Canadian (or the New York) clock for a long time. But sport crystallizes popular opinion, and this antagonism towards "the East" was vehement, and almost a reflex. And it was about more than hockey and clocks. I have run into too many flash points like that in the last few years in Canada. There are parts of the country where seeds of anger and resentment have been germinating out of the sight of national observers but which are ready to burst into view. It is rarely pleasant to see anger blossom, but we need to know it's there to root it out. Ironically, by forcing us to recognize that we can't continue business as usual, the so-called constitutional issue may cause us to face the more basic question of Canadian purpose.

I began noting down some of these reflections during the constitutional process itself. I thought it part of my responsibility to talk to Canadians about the nature and history of the country whose constitution we were proposing to change, and some of those observations are repeated in this book. In my year away, I have had time to reflect more upon the nature and future of our country.

I think we underestimate both the value of Canada and the danger of allowing it to drift apart. In my view, the real challenge is not from separatism in Quebec, but from a sense of indifference in the country at large – a sense either that things will take care of themselves or, more starkly, that, if they do not, it won't matter much.

That is by no means a majority view in Canada now. Thousands, probably millions, of Canadians have become more self-consciously patriotic in the last few years. More Canadian flags are flown. In English-speaking Canada, more advertisements consciously strike Canadian themes. The *Maclean's*/ Decima poll published on July 1, 1994, reported that a startling 96 per cent of Canadian respondents believe Canada is the best country in the world in which to live. But those are mere surface signs, and no one knows whether they can be translated into support for changes that might be needed to make the nation work.

The danger is that indifference is also addictive, and busy people, distracted by other concerns, could buy into the argument that the alarums about the future of Canada are false. Many of those activist Canadians who could normally be called upon to come to the aid of their country may acquiesce in the view that Canada isn't really threatened, or, worse, that it doesn't really matter.

Ironically, precisely the opposite attitude is developing in Quebec. To Quebecers, their society matters, their community is important. If the contest there is between an indifferent Canada and a proud Quebec, independence will win.

So, in my view, the real questions are whether we can summon a sense of Canadian purpose, and, if so, whether that purpose would be strong enough to engage Quebecers too. I think the answer to both of those questions is yes, precisely because this is such an accomplished and valuable country. Canada is, literally, too good to lose, but we have to work at building and keeping it.

In the spring of 1956, I got on the train in Calgary, to come to Ottawa, as part of the "Adventure in Citizenship" program run by the Rotary Club. New kids came aboard at every stop. We were all sixteen or seventeen, and sat up all night in the CPR's "dome cars," watching the prairie roll by and then the Canadian Shield, and then crossing into Hull before we came to Ottawa. Our first conscious view of the capital was the Centre Block, home to the House of Commons, standing tall on Parliament Hill.

I had never been east of Medicine Hat before that trip; but, in the years since, I have probably been in more Canadian places, large and small, than most people have heard of. I tried to be especially vigilant during my travels; after all, I was not a tourist, Canada was my business, and I needed to understand how it felt to live in Newfoundland, or to work a trap line out of Old Crow, or to teach in downtown Montreal in a school whose students spoke twenty different languages when they went home to their parents. Part of the privilege of being a politician in Canada is that, generally, people welcome you into their communities, and want you to understand who they are, and why.

What I have learned, across those years, from Mistassini to Spadina, to the Saint John shipyards, to the Stoney Reserve, confirms my view that we Canadians are the luckiest of people, not only because of the wealth and beauty of our land, but also because of the communities we have built here, the local communities where we are rooted and the national community where we can grow. Sometimes those local communities are actual places – towns, villages, neighbourhoods – but just as often they are schools or credit unions or the Chinese Benevolent Society. There is enormous strength in those communities, and pride, generosity, ingenuity.

To a remarkable degree, in Canada, most of those communities have purposes that are more than material. And they are bound together by positive feelings, not anger, not envy, not fear. That doesn't happen everywhere in this world.

In almost all of those local communities, there is a consistent respect for Canada, and, particularly among new Canadians, a gratitude for the country. But how deep is that respect, and how intensely is it felt? As a practical matter, what will it mean if there is a pull between local interests and the larger Canada?

Something is missing. The Canada that foreigners admire, that refugees risk their lives to come to, has lost its emotional hold on many of its own people. The connections that draw together the members of our local communities don't extend farther, to reach to the whole country. Instead, more Canadians are focusing narrowly – as Quebecers, as Albertans, as aboriginals.

I think the problem is more than one of size or distance or diversity. Other large countries – France, the United States, Britain, to name three that mark our history – seem to excite more emotion among their nationals than Canada does among Canadians. Yet we can make a better case: we have more strengths; more advantages; more space, both geographic and personal.

I believe the reason is straightforward: we have not tried hard enough to know our Canadian neighbours. We do not understand what drives them to do things differently than we do. Obviously, there are some exceptions, some Canadians who make it a point to watch the news and read the literature of other regions, and visit and stay long enough to learn something. But most Canadians have not been to another part of Canada. Most Quebecers do not travel to Alberta, nor most Albertans to Quebec. And now that the warning flags are up, and there is a full-blown separatist movement in Quebec and a fledgling rejectionist movement in Alberta, travellers are on their guard. They go to other regions like scientists investigating a species, rather than like neighbours visiting another part of their town.

Is this too simple an explanation? I don't think so. Other countries are torn by hatred, or historical divisions, or religion, or desperation. Not Canada. On the contrary: when Canadians actually get together, we usually agree on fundamental questions. We are not natural enemies. In fact, when we meet, friendships develop easily.

I am not pretending Canada is free of serious differences and disagreements. That is part of life everywhere. Clearly, the issues of language and money and jurisdiction will always be contentious in Canada. The point is that they are not life-threatening differences, such as bedevil truly divided societies, and we should not pretend that they are.

Part of my purpose here is to create some common understanding of the reasons why some Canadians are seeking changes. Quite apart from our differences about solutions, we Canadians do not have a common view of what our problems are, because not many of us know very much about our neighbours. We are the second-largest country in the world, and that distance gets in our way. Most Canadians probably understand in a general way that there is a problem in Quebec, a problem with Native people, and something wrong in the West. But those are not tangible problems that we experience in a real way, like pressures at work or potholes in the road.

Most of us have never met a Native leader, or a Quebec nationalist, or an advocate of a "Triple-E" Senate. What are passionate causes to some Canadians are just phrases to most others – and, often, those phrases are codewords for "trouble." I have had to learn those codes, and interpret the communities they come from, so I could work with all of them. My strong conclusion is that, while the codewords might sound alarming, the actual causes they purport to describe should neither frighten nor divide Canadians. But it is human nature to fear what we don't know, so this book tries to get behind the codes and provide a simple description of the motives which drive demands for change. Once we have a common basis for interpreting our country and its challenges, we will have a better chance to take considered decisions together.

This book has been published in a French edition as well and, naturally, I hope it will interest Canadians everywhere. But the principal audience I seek to address is outside Quebec. Obviously, the next questions about Canada are likely to be raised in that province, where there is an active separatist movement. But, in my view, the most important answers about Canada must come from citizens in the rest of the country.

For years now – at least since René Lévesque mobilized the Parti Québécois – large numbers of contemporary Quebecers have been thinking seriously about the country they want to be. By contrast, the rest of the country has considered those questions only when Quebec raises them. Our assumption has been that the country was working reasonably well, and "if it ain't broke, don't fix it."

There has been serious thought and argument about specific issues and proposals, like foreign investment, the Free Trade Agreement, child care. But there has not been a broad and energetic consideration of our goals as a country. For some time, our focus was on the unity of the country, not its purpose. We wanted to "save Canada" without giving much thought to what Canada is, or what it could become.

The modern Quebec independence movement is rooted in the historic nationalism of that province, and a self-consciousness that is natural to a community which, despite its strength, still knows that it is a minority. But it has grown beyond those origins, to become an instrument with which to design a future.

That is where the larger Canada has missed an opportunity.

The arguments against independence are couched in terms of economics and stability and mutual advantage. I happen to believe that most of those arguments are valid. But they do not address the sense of goals and purpose that has become associated with the idea of independence. They are too pragmatic. They evoke a deal, not a dream.

It is not surprising that the Canadian response should be pragmatic. That is true to our character, and our history. Our success in building this large and diverse country has depended upon common sense, perseverance, compromise – those sturdy Canadian qualities.

But that success has also required some sense of vision – the idea of a large nation, not a small one, *a mare usque ad mare*, stretching physically from the Atlantic to the Pacific, then to the Arctic, and, in terms of its possibilities, stretching into infinity. John A. Macdonald and Wilfrid Laurier evoked that sense, and so, at their best, did John Diefenbaker, in 1958, and Pierre Trudeau, a decade later.

That happened, of course, in a less cynical time. The modern age is hard on vision, sceptical of dreams and grand designs. Yet, paradoxically, there is a search for purpose, and it tests all institutions – churches, corporations, universities, nations.

The irony is that no country in the world offers more to dream about, more to aspire to, than Canada. Residents of other cities in North America envy the cleanliness and safety and vitality of Toronto and Vancouver and other Canadian cities. Our citizens are protected against the fear that sudden illness could also bring the shock of impossible costs. Our respect for equality is sufficiently strong that, when the United Nations judged that our Indian Act violated the rights of aboriginal women, we changed the Indian Act, despite the protest of many chiefs and tribal councils. These are not random or unrelated realities about Canada. They reflect a consistent commitment to a superior quality of life. It is no small accomplishment for a nation to be celebrated for the way it treats its citizens. But that is only half the story.

Canada has become a creative, dynamic community – in music, in technology, in diplomacy, in the fields of the future, Canadians are innovators and leaders. It was once our lot to hew wood and draw water, and live in the shadow of the French, or the British, or the Americans. But Canada today is moving out of those shadows, and we are winning respect on our own.

And those are the results of community, not geography; of accomplishment, not luck. Canada is respected now for what its citizens have done and not just the wealth we found in our ground. That is directly relevant to the debate about Canada's future. We have developed a momentum in Canada. Our industries and artists and society are reaching outward, building a future. That momentum is itself creative. It is a Canadian asset, which we should prize, not put at risk. Yet, if the country comes apart – with a whimper or a bang – that asset would be gone. We would become a country to feel sorry for, rather than to take seriously. And, in my view, we would be plunged into the most bitter of debates at home, about how we would divide a debt, or settle boundaries, or renegotiate international treaties and agreements.

The alternative to drifting apart is to join together to build on the sense of a Canada that is coming into its own. We are a country unlike any other in the world, with the most exciting of possibilities, but undeniable and serious tensions within our own community. Clearly the old ways of dealing with those tensions won't work, at least in the short term. That was one of the lessons of the 1992 referendum. But there is no point pretending that the issues which have divided us will go away if we ignore them. In a strict sense, those issues are "constitutional," but the real question is whether the different communities in Canada have the will to live together. So let us begin to focus on what that means, in a Canada entering a new millennium. The old debate was about "unity," about how we could stay together, and it became counterproductive. The new debate should be about goals and purposes, what we can do together, to make the most of our uniquely diverse Canadian community.

One of the ironies of public life is that I may have more standing out of office than I did as a minister and parliamentarian. There has always been cynicism about politics, but it became particularly pernicious in the early 1990s. Critics who had previously questioned only the judgement, or the competence, of politicians began increasingly to question their motives and character. Putting aside, for the moment, the question of why that happened, the result was to reduce the authority of public office, and that was a particular burden when your job was to build consensus. And, in any event, there is a certain advantage to being out of the arena. Robert Stanfield has observed that no one is more honoured than a former Conservative leader, and I have noticed that the government I led in 1979 was far more popular in retrospect than it ever was in office.

Many Canadians know our country, and several understand the particular communities they come from better than I ever will. But I have had the unusual opportunity to see it whole, from the inside, as the leader of a party and a government striving to be national, and from the outside, as an active foreign minister, who worked every day with countries that were less successful than Canada, and with people who envied what we had, or admired what we had done.

I do not defend the country simply because it is here, but

because I genuinely believe that the Canadian way of respecting different communities and identities is more successful than the approaches of other countries and, indeed, is a model for the world of the future. Many Canadians know American history, and the history of other countries, better than they know our own. That is lamentable, because that is to choose the excitement of battles and conquests over the success of building a peaceful and prosperous community. The more violent history of other societies is relevant to us mainly because we avoided it. In 1865, George Brown, who was to become a pivotal founder of the Canadian federation, looked south, to a nation torn between its Unionist North and its Confederate South, and then looked around him, to the colonies considering Confederation, communities with different economic interests, different languages, different laws and traditions. Reflecting on the Confederation he was helping to achieve, George Brown observed: "We are endeavouring to adjust harmoniously greater difficulties than have plunged other countries into all the horrors of civil war. . . . Have we not then great cause of thankfulness that we have found a better way for the solution of our troubles . . . ?" His assessment of Canada as "the better way" is more apt now than ever.

The brief chapters that follow describe our country, as I have come to know it, and our problems, as I understand them. I hope this book might serve as a catalyst in encouraging other Canadians to build this remarkable country, rather than have it break, or drift apart.

TWO

THE VIEW FROM
HIGH RIVER

MANY PEOPLE BELIEVE THERE IS NO THREAT TO CANADA'S FUTURE,
or no solution to its historical tensions, or no time to do anything about them. They are reconciled to drifting into whatever
the future holds. I simply disagree with those who see no threat,
whether they hold the sceptical view that Canada's crises are
always exaggerated, or they have come to believe that we would
be better off ending the Canadian experiment. But I am acutely
aware that time is short, and that what we face is a question
about more than the constitution. It is about a country – my
country – and about a national community which is a marked
success, and worth preserving and building upon.

I write as a Canadian raised in Alberta, and shaped by a
unique experience in Canadian and international affairs. I have
had the privilege of seeing how Canada's different interests
connect – how we function both as particular self-conscious

communities and as what I have referred to as a Canadian "community of communities" whose larger interests draw us ultimately together. In one sense, I make no claim to be objective, because I have been very close to these issues, and clearly want Canada to stay together. My hope is that my perspective may help other Canadians see this extraordinary community in its larger context.

Of course, I am conscious of the new deadlines looming in Quebec. I understand the argument of some Quebecers that this is now a debate from which the rest of the country should stand back. I respect Quebec's right to make its own decisions and, indeed, to decide to separate from Canada. But Canada is *my* business too, and I have a right, and an obligation, to try to persuade Canadians everywhere that it is better to keep and change the country than to split it forever into angry parts.

My experience has convinced me that, when Canadians take one another seriously and actually listen to what is being said, we can agree. But it is harder now to bring Canadians to a common starting place. We are driven by different experiences, and increasingly define ourselves as separate from one another. Naturally, if we see ourselves as separate, the country will become divided. My hope is that we might still come to look at what we have in common, what we have to gain, and lose, as individuals and as communities.

I bring a very particular perspective to these issues, not simply because I had the good fortune to serve in the national Parliament and government, but because of what I learned growing up. For nearly sixty years, my father, and his father, ran weekly newspapers in southern Alberta, in the little towns of Okotoks, Vulcan, and, principally, High River.

Much more than is the case today, weekly newspapers then

were at the core of the community. In economic terms, they were never as important as the farms and ranches and small businesses which generated jobs and produce. In fact, our newspapers could barely be considered commercial ventures, because they rarely made money, and were kept afloat by using our presses to print brochures and auction sheets and wedding invitations. But our weekly newspapers were the memory and the membrane of the community, keeping track of births and deaths and successes and failures, and connecting the community, helping it be whole. I have been lucky in a lot of life, including growing up in a place like High River, where we tried to see things whole.

My grandfather came west from Bruce County, in the late 1800s, on a "press tour." His brother published a newspaper in Kincardine, Ontario, and so could send kin on adventures to what were then the North-West Territories. Several times during my constitutional consultations, when I encountered the simple ignorance our regions have of one another, I wondered why those "press tours" had stopped, and how we might start them again. In any event, my grandfather filed his reports, went off to the Boer War, and then came back to the foothills of what would soon be Alberta.

His first venture was raising horses west of Okotoks and, when that didn't work, he took over *The Okotoks Review*, in a little community on the Sheep River, south of Calgary. In those early days, all type was set by hand, and *The Review*'s owner, Sam Hodgson, had become frustrated, thrown all the type in the corner of the shop, and sold his business. My grandfather spent his first weeks as an Alberta journalist patiently sorting out and cleaning the type.

Sixteen kilometres to the south, in High River, the local

paper was called *The Eye Opener*, and its editor was Bob Edwards, who was as close as Canada came to a Mark Twain. The news was not enough for Edwards, so he enlivened it, inventing characters like "Albert Buzzard-Cholomondeley," a British remittance man, whose letters home for funds ran regularly in *The Eye Opener*. So did social notes, one sample of which (from the later *Calgary Eye Opener*) was: "Miss Maude de Vere, of Drumheller, arrived in the city Wednesday and was run out of town the same night. It is a pity that Miss de Vere is not a racehorse, for she is very fast."

It may not be true to say that Edwards was himself run out of High River, but, at the least, he was not encouraged to stay. A local church had decided to supplement its choir with records being hawked by a travelling gramophone salesman. On the Sunday morning of the demonstration, someone switched the records, and the congregation was treated to: "Just Because She Made Them Goo-Goo Eyes." No one could prove it was Edwards but, a few nights later, he showed up in my grandfather's shop and said: "Charlie, I think there's an opening in High River."

The first edition of *The High River Times* appeared in December 1905, the year Alberta became a province. With rare exceptions, it has published every week since, regularly winning newspaper awards, and recording the life and growth of a community.

My family reported the meetings, wrote the stories, sold the advertisements, set the type, took the pictures. For a while, because he had to report on, and thus attend, each of their meetings, my father was a member of both the Knights of Columbus and the Masonic Lodge in High River. That pretty well spanned the range of southern Alberta diversity at that simpler time.

But if the community was less complex, the coverage was both more intimate and more complete. If you think of the old country doctor who made house calls, you have some sense of how a good weekly newspaper reached into its community then. Journalism now is more adversarial, and journalists prize their distance from what they report. The best weeklies were the opposite – they got inside the community and interpreted it for itself, reporting not just the "news" but the texture.

Of course, in order to interpret and reflect the community, you had to understand it, respect it. Looking back, that was an ideal preparation for public life. I grew up inquiring why the stores were closed on Wednesday afternoons (the merchants had to go to Calgary to restock) and open Saturday nights (the farm families came in to shop); which of the Catholic families were sensitive about the Protestants, and vice versa; why the owner of the Chinese café had so many nephews who would show up in his kitchen, cook a while, and then move on; and who was likely to know what about whom.

For more than thirty years, a woman named Hughena McCorquodale worked at *The Times*. Her title was "editor"; her genius was empathy and a remarkable ability to draw people out. In another place, with a meaner spirit, she would have been Hedda Hopper or Walter Winchell.

A staple of *The Times* was "the locals," a weekly record of who visited, who travelled, whose son came second in the tenor competition of the Crows Nest Pass Musical Festival. It was less gossip than glue. It kept the community up to date about its members, and Mrs. McCorquodale had an amazing reach and talent.

One unusual summer, she took two weeks' holiday, and I was entrusted to write "the locals." I was seventeen, and this was going to be a snap – just phone up her list of names, ask what was happening, and write it down. Her "sources" were all polite, and gave me "the facts," and I produced two weeks' worth of the dullest "locals" in the history of *The High River Times*. I didn't understand the relations, couldn't put my snippets of fact in any context. Writing "the locals" was more complex than just recording who came and went. Mrs. McCorquodale's "locals" gave you a sense of how the facts fit together, how the community connected.

Communities have to connect, and the way they do it is rarely straightforward or on the surface. If that was challenging in a small and homogeneous place like High River in the 1950s, think how much more so it is in 1994, in the sprawling and diverse community that is Canada.

And it is the connections which are breaking in Canada. The lines are not yet down among our Canadian communities, but they are in bad repair, and we have lost or let wither much of our sense of interdependence. We are acting as though we can close the gates against our neighbours, yet keep the friendships.

THREE

A COMMUNITY OF COMMUNITIES

I HAVE DESCRIBED CANADA AS A "COMMUNITY OF COMMUNITIES" because that is how I have experienced it. High River was more than a tangible place. You knew your neighbours, and you cared about them, even those you might not like or know well.

But you knew you were part of a larger whole. The wheat and cattle our neighbours raised weren't all eaten at home. They went somewhere, and money came back that was spent on tractors or radios or grapefruit that were produced somewhere else. And when those goods were sold in our foothills, they were advertised in *The High River Times*, which, my dad reminded us, was how we could afford a bicycle or a baseball glove.

To a youngster growing up in the 1940s, when the sixty-kilometre drive to Calgary was a long way and there was no television, that wide world was pretty indistinct. Sometimes, of course, it could intrude sharply. One of my early memories is of neighbours crowding into our house because my father's short-wave radio could pick up the Great Falls station, which was broadcasting live the fight for the "Heavyweight Championship of the World" ("the World"!), between Joe Louis and Billy Conn. More tragically, I remember the day, in 1945, when the phone rang in our kitchen to tell my Aunt Geg that her oldest son had died in Europe, just as the Second World War was ending.

There were no formal "Welcome Wagons" then, but if someone fell sick, neighbours would come by with food or offers to take the children for the night. I have a flickering childhood memory of a building bee, on a farm near Aldersyde. The farmer had broken his leg in a fall from a barn he was building, and his neighbours both finished the barn and took off his crop. Those "locals" in *The High River Times*, which Mrs. McCorquodale drew so effortlessly from her network, were not gossip about strangers, served up to wound, but family news, as natural and binding as conversations across a backyard fence.

That town was small, and fairly homogeneous. Almost everyone was white, English-speaking, and Christian. But even that Christianity was far from uniform. When I was in high school, the town population was about 1800, and counted 22 separate churches. That included neither the congregations that met in homes, nor those who gathered to hear itinerant evangelists, who were always numerous in summer. And it did not take account of divisions within congregations, such as the sharp dispute in my own Roman Catholic church between those who wanted a separate school and people like my father who prevailed with the argument that separate schools split small towns. The seamless fraternity of the Christian faith aside, the town had enough differences and disagreements to keep things lively.

High River always saw itself as a special place, and I would guess that most of the people who lived there for long still have that sense.

That was a positive definition of place, not against the otherness of anywhere else, but a quiet identification with a set of experiences and scenery and values – with the spectacular vista westward to the Rocky Mountains, the relative harmony among its citizens, the sense of special worth that attaches to farming towns, and the annual community events, such as "Amateur Night" when all the youngsters, in solo performances or duets or small groups, sang contemporary songs (often the same contemporary song: My brother, Peter, and I were one of at least thirty entrants who offered our version of "Mockingbird Hill" one interminable spring evening) or the Roman Catholic Midnight Mass, sung then in Latin, by a choir which recruited actively from several of the twenty-one other churches in town.

I used to think High River had the patent on that sense of being a place, a base, a defining community. But Canada is rooted in communities like that, places which, while you might leave them, keep drawing you back, at least emotionally, and sometimes physically. People from Cape Breton may live now around the country, or around the world, but where they are from is Cape Breton – North Sydney or Glace Bay or Baddeck. The same is true of Newfoundland and, to a greater or lesser degree, all of Atlantic Canada, and most of the communities I know in the rest of the country.

And it is as much an urban as a rural phenomenon. David Crombie has written similarly of Swansea, where he grew up, and would say that particular community – which was part of, yet apart from, the larger metropolis of Toronto – shaped his view of his country, our country, as surely as High River shaped mine. The north end of Winnipeg left a defining imprint on the people who were raised there, as did other urban neighbourhoods, from Boyle Street to Kitsilano, to Saint Urbain. Benoît Bouchard draws a large part of his sense of himself from Lac Saint-Jean, as, I am sure, Jean Chrétien does from Shawinigan.

What is interesting to me is not that individuals have roots which are important to them, because I presume that happens everywhere, but that the roots in Canada are to communities, not just families — to, if I might stretch a point, a neighbourhood, not a log cabin.

The Glebe, in Ottawa, where two generations of McTeers were raised, was so cohesive a community that, when Maureen's late father showed up with a son-in-law who thought he would like to lead a political party, my improbable campaign suddenly became a community project, in a place that was far from my base, but just a strategic two blocks from the hall where the convention would be held. That was one illustration — rather important to me — of the reality that this local pride, this local identity, need not be confining. It can reach out, because it is based on a proven sense of security and definition.

That local identity is durable and real across Canada. It has the double advantage of being home-grown and, sometimes, having been forged in difficult circumstances. Part of the reason that Atlantic Canada has been able to withstand the dramatic changes in its economic circumstances is the widely held belief, among the people who were raised there, in the worth of their communities. Pride became a kind of currency, and led Atlantic Canadians to build strong and modern universities and institutions and industries, despite economic pressures.

That sense of pride can itself become a tangible asset. One of the most successful international meetings I attended was the 1986 meeting of Foreign Ministers of the North Atlantic Treaty

Organization (NATO) in Halifax. What made the difference was the evident pride of Nova Scotians in their maritime and military traditions. The welcoming atmosphere in the province affected the discussions themselves, which were more lively and frank than usual. For years afterwards, I ran into NATO ministers or officials who told me the Halifax meeting was the best of its kind.

The ties that connect Canadians to their larger community are not as strong, or as personal. Local pride comes naturally, but Canadian patriotism is an acquired taste, something you have to work up deliberately. In comparable large democracies – the United States, France, Britain – national myths and symbols carry as much emotional charge as local loyalties, but not in Canada.

We think of provinces or regions – large entities – when we consider the strong local loyalties that might frustrate pan-Canadian ventures, or might be mobilized to animate a sense of pan-Canadian community. But often the root of that pride and identity is in smaller, more local, communities.

In the case of Quebec, whose distinct society is province-wide, a lot of the identification is with the large Quebec community. But within that, there are more local loyalties. The communities of the Beauce, south of Quebec City, are as different from Montreal as Vegreville is from Calgary. The rugged and beautiful landscapes of Saguenay-Lac Saint-Jean have disproportionately been the source of Quebec nationalism and constructive myth. Rouyn-Noranda, and other towns of the northwest of the province, have almost a Western Canadian rhythm in their streets and life. Those communities, and others like them, are the places from which distinctive parts of Quebec's identity spring. And that is to mention only communities which are predominantly francophone and, in some cases, almost exclusively so. It says nothing of the aboriginal people, or the old English-language communities

in the Townships or Western Quebec or Montreal or along the
Gaspé coast, or of the communities from Greece or Italy or Haiti
or the Ukraine or a hundred other societies now planted deeply
in Quebec. They are not pawns in this game about the future of
Quebec, and it is important to consider whether, in fact, those
smaller communities would be better able to maintain their identity, their pride, in a separate Quebec, which will have to be built
anew, or in a fundamental renewal of the Canadian federation.

Two large communities associated with Quebec would
become extremely uneasy – fundamentally insecure – with separation. Obviously, that would be the case with those communities in Quebec whose citizens are not primarily French-
speaking. There has been an English-speaking population in
Quebec for centuries, and many of its members cannot separate
their identities as Quebecers and as Canadians because they have
been both for generations. A few are separatists, and many more
have been in the vanguard of constitutional reforms which
would guarantee Quebec's "distinct society" within Canada.
Some others will never come to terms with Quebec nationalism, which they see principally as a threat to themselves.

If there is a referendum, all the evidence points to the like-
lihood that those communities – the so-called allophone and
anglophone communities – would vote strongly for Canada,
against separation, and that, if separation prevailed, they would
be uneasy and threatened. The great majority of that population
lives in the Montreal region, an urban multicultural metropolis, whose difference from the rest of Quebec is already accen-
tuated by slow growth and high unemployment.

There would also be great concern among French-speaking Canadians who live outside Quebec. Some of those francophone communities are anchored in fairly large centres –

Moncton, Sudbury, St. Boniface, and others – but several are dispersed throughout little places – Maillardville in B.C., Falher in Alberta, Gravelbourg in Saskatchewan, southwestern Nova Scotia, and communities scattered from the Yukon to P.E.I., to the counties of eastern Ontario, where the McTeers were the only English-speaking family in their country school. The survival of those French-speaking communities, outside Quebec, has depended upon two forces working together – one is the simple existence of the large French-speaking community of Quebec, which is proof that the culture can survive; the other has been the requirement, by Canada, that French-language minorities be respected. Separatist leaders offer soothing assurances to Canadian francophones outside Quebec, but they cannot mask the reality that, one way or another, those French-speaking minorities would be victims if Quebec separates. Even with the best will in the world, governments in what remained of Canada would find it very difficult to maintain their support for francophone minorities.

Within Quebec, separation would not mean an escape from the necessity, and the frustrations, of working with, and accommodating, very different groups. To state the starkest problem first, the claims of aboriginal people would not diminish; on the contrary, and for various reasons, the prospect of Quebec separation would likely make those differences and tensions more acute, more quickly. To a greater or lesser degree, other minorities who suddenly felt themselves deprived of the protection of Canada would experience a similar anxiety and assertiveness. Separatist leaders are quick to agree that an independent Quebec will not step back to some simple or mythic time. However, the point is not just that an independent Quebec would be as complex as it is today, but rather that the very prospect and act of separation would add to the complexity and tension. Ironically, in order to succeed, an independent Quebec would have to become much more like Canada – that is, a community of communities itself. Even then, an acceptable level of harmony among very different Quebec communities may, in fact, be harder to accomplish in a new experiment, where tensions are bound to be high, than it would be in a large federation which has had considerable success in respecting and harmonizing diversity.

FOUR

TAKING CANADA
FOR GRANTED

CANADA IS A LUCKY AND VALUABLE COUNTRY AND, IRONICALLY,
that is part of our problem. We take for granted the growth,
tolerance, and relative serenity of this peaceable kingdom, and
assume those advantages would survive any shock.

The trouble with luck is that you come to count on it. You
forget how it was earned. Canada has immense natural advantages – resources, location, space. Yet our success as a country
is a result of what we did with those advantages. Our prosperity, our social programs, and our remarkable tolerance as a community were built by Canadians who took nothing for granted,
and who understood that the integrity of our country was the
fundamental asset upon which other advantages depended.

I have just spent a year living and working in the United States.
In that country, 37 million Americans – almost 10 million more
people than in all of Canada – have no health care insurance.

Universal access to quality health care is part of the definition of Canada. We put in practice the belief that a person's financial status should not determine his or her entitlement to necessary medical services. Canadians worry often about losing our identity to our powerful neighbour. In fact, on important questions, the influence is the other way; we are already the "kinder, gentler" society which former president George Bush urged his nation to become.

But my point is not just that the value we place on the quality of our collective lives is a uniquely Canadian attribute. It is also that it is the premise upon which we have built and strengthened our communities over the years. The systems which ensure that quality of life were not an accident in Canada. We built our systems of health care and social programs ourselves. We chose and designed those models deliberately, to suit this special country, and we are working today to improve them.

I am surprised by the number of Canadians now who seem to assume that our prosperity, our social programs, and our tolerance will stay intact even if our country comes apart. The Canadian assumption is that we are somehow protected here, by our geography or our physical wealth or the sophisticated nature of our trading relations or our skill levels. For Canadians, the really awful things happen elsewhere in the world. In Quebec City, as in Calgary, we think we have a lot of latitude.

That is a dangerous illusion. The threat to Canada is both serious and urgent and, if we allow the country to break up, the harm will be immediate and lasting to Canadians everywhere — in the West and Atlantic Canada, in Ontario and the North, as well as in Quebec.

More than in most countries, in Canada prosperity is tied to our reputation in the world. We have already lost some of our relative advantage, because we responded slowly to economic changes elsewhere. The European Community took traditional Canadian agricultural markets. The new Asian economies took traditional Canadian manufacturing markets.

Of course, our natural wealth is an immense advantage, and our skill levels can be, but other countries also have resources and skills. More than we admit, Canada depends upon a reputation of stability, and upon international agreements that were signed between foreign countries and a Canada that is whole.

No one who was involved in the negotiation of the Free Trade Agreement, as I was, would doubt that, if Canada broke up, the United States would move very quickly to renegotiate that agreement, and would seek new terms detrimental to the interests of any Canadians who had something the Americans wanted, whether those people live in what is now Quebec or in what is now Alberta. That reaction by the United States would have nothing to do with its regard for Canada or, indeed, its position on an independent Quebec. The reality is that Americans will always pursue their own interests. Sometimes those are genuine national interests, initiated by a president or an administration, but often they are very local, even eccentric, triggered by a particular congressman or senator whose power the president cannot override.

Anyone who doubts that the United States would use separation as an excuse to renegotiate the Free Trade Agreement needs only to remember what went on during the original negotiation. Senators Max Baucus, of Montana, and Robert Packwood, of Oregon, fiercely opposed the agreement because they wanted more advantages for the U.S. lumber industry. Senator John Danforth, of Missouri, and Congressman John Dingell, of Michigan, among others, opposed the cultural exemption that was so important for Canada. Senator George Mitchell, of Maine, the majority leader in the Senate, voted against the agreement for several reasons, but one of them was to protect the lobster industry in his home state. I refer to those legislators because their targets, by and large, were not in Quebec. There is also a long list of Americans who are very unhappy with support in the agreement for the dairy industry, and for resource development, and for other trade-related issues that are important to Quebec. That makes the point that a renegotiation, from a position of profound weakness, would be very bad news for Canadians everywhere. Those U.S. senators and congressmen lost their case last time, but it is absolutely certain that they, or their successors, would make a stronger case once troubles in Canada gave them an excuse to reopen the agreement.

Two other lessons from that period should be considered by any Canadian who would acquiesce in the break-up of Canada. First, once agreements are opened, they become hostages to a very unpredictable Congress. In order to have the Free Trade Agreement dealt with quickly, on the so-called fast track, we needed at least a tie vote in a twenty-member Senate committee. We barely got a tie – ten to ten. And one of the votes against the Free Trade Agreement had nothing at all to do with Canada or free trade; the dissenting senator was unhappy with U.S. State Department policy respecting products alleged to have been manufactured by slave labour in the then-Soviet Union.

The second lesson is more current. When President Clinton needed votes to carry NAFTA, the North American Free Trade Agreement, he won the support of key senators by promising to get tougher with Canadians about wheat. That is the real reason Canadian wheat producers are under U.S. pressure now. Both lessons demonstrate that, at the best of times, one should not casually reopen negotiations with the United States. That would be even more the case if the new negotiation were to be between a superpower and two diminished communities recovering from separation.

When Canada defends our international economic interests now, we do so as a relatively powerful country, one of only seven nations who participate in the annual Economic Summit, and a nation which enjoys an enviable reputation for stability in a turbulent world.

Does that help us in the give-and-take of a negotiation? Would we be better off as a smaller power, outside the G-7? Are the investment houses which assign credit ratings to Saskatchewan or Manitoba or Nova Scotia or Newfoundland likely to give as high a rating to part of a divided country? What about Quebec's credit rating, particularly if its rich land base is challenged by aboriginal people, or if it has to assume a larger share of the Canadian debt?

There has not been much detailed debate about the costs of dividing Canada, in part because attempts to raise that issue have triggered accusations of fear-mongering, and in part because of a natural reluctance to speculate publicly on failure. But there are costs. Anyone who has moved from a large house to a smaller one knows that. So does anyone whose income has dropped. Canada's house would be smaller. Our income would plummet.

That has consequences beyond the economy. Canadian prosperity is the only guarantee that Canadian social programs will continue. You can't pay for pensions and medicare and equalization with goodwill. If separation hurts Canada's economy, the social benefits which our citizens everywhere have come to count on will be eroded. No one should assume that the advantages of a large country would pass automatically to two smaller ones.

As usual, the poorest regions of Canada would suffer first, and most seriously. For example, the separation of Quebec would be a terrible blow to Atlantic Canada. Not only would it be cut off physically from the rest of the country, but its citizens would have to contemplate the prospect that radical surgery on Canada's geography would lead naturally to a change in the traditional commitment of richer regions to help the poorer, through equalization and transfer payments. Atlantic Canada's ability to borrow, or to attract investment, would be quickly and directly threatened by a separation that left it hanging out on the end.

While the problem is most graphic in relation to Atlantic Canada, similar pressures may face remote regions of other provinces. Part of the Canadian tradition has been for regions with more population and income to help offset the disadvantages of remote and smaller communities, through support for hospitals, highways, and other services. No one can know whether that tradition would survive the failure of the Canadian idea of a large land in which every citizen had a stake, but, if that commitment withers, what, for example, is the interest of multicultural, metropolitan southward-looking Toronto in the mining communities or Native bands or smaller towns in the northern parts of Ontario?

In the twinkle of an eye, we could start a spiral down into a divided and deeply troubled community. In some countries, which were built or sustained by fiat, that kind of disintegration may be inevitable, but that is not the case in Canada. Confederation was not forced on any of the provinces. It has been a remarkably flexible system, taking account of the differences that necessarily exist in a large country. While there are disagreements and some divisions in our diverse community, our real differences are not profound, and certainly not worth break-ing up over.

Time is against Canada. Yet another referendum is looming in Quebec, and it could pull the thread that unravels the country. Whatever the words of a referendum question, the issue will be whether Canada is attractive enough to Quebecers that they will want to help build the larger community of Canada and not just the close-knit community of Quebec.

At the same time, in the rest of the country, there is a real and growing resentment of the idea that Canada's agenda is being driven by Quebec. That resentment is not inherently anti-Quebec, although it has stoked that sentiment. Seen more con-structively, it is a demand that the urgent priorities of other Canadians be given serious attention too, and not be short-changed by a pre-occupation with Quebec.

In the wider world, this is an age when things come apart. Traditional authority is losing its sure grip – in churches, in fam-ilies, and in several countries besides Canada. Other countries, however, have more help in adapting to those modern centrifugal forces. Their territory is smaller, and, usually, their population more homogeneous. But they are also sustained by their national myths, which are more powerful, and more personal, than ours. For example, for most citizens of France, "La Marseillaise" is a personal anthem, a direct connection with their history, their revolution, their sense of themselves. In the United States, in China, in Italy, in Australia – in most countries – the sense of identity is similarly strong and tangible.

Canada's boast has been that we have "a quiet sense of our-selves." But that proud diffidence should not become an excuse for letting the country slip away.

A "quiet sense" served us very well in a time when nothing

seemed to challenge Canada. For a long time, after the Second World War, we thought we had good reason to take things for granted. The Canadian universe was unfolding as it should. Today we are paying for that comfortable illusion, and paying on several accounts. The debt which haunts every government was built in those free-spending days when we assumed our growth would forever sustain our ambitions. The neglect of our Native people – and, indeed, their abuse by teachers and churches and other institutions they were told they could most trust – incubated the despair and resentment we have to face today. The comfort we found in tariffs and other protections lulled us into falling behind countries – mainly in Asia, but also in the new Europe of the Common Market – whose whole purpose was to become better educated, more competitive. The steady economic growth of Ontario muted questions about whether our economic assumptions, and political systems, were working as well as we thought they were.

And, now, suddenly, Canada is being challenged, seriously and on several fronts – by foreign competitors, by a strait-jacket of debt, and by separatist and other pressures at home. In those circumstances, a "quiet sense of ourselves" isn't enough. We are paying a price now for that vaunted Canadian modesty which has led us to give too little attention to our history and our achievements, at home and in the world.

That has all been made more serious by a change in the self-confidence of Ontario. Whether other Canadians liked it or not, Ontario has traditionally assumed a role as the ballast in Canada. It was the reliable engine of economic growth, the steady hand in relations between the national government and more fractious provinces, the solid centre of the country. Other regions often resented the pervasive dominance of Ontario, and that resentment itself nourished the tensions in Confederation, but, traditionally, Ontario itself seemed untroubled either by that resentment or by the assumption that it has special responsibilities as the richest, largest province.

As a young leader of the opposition, in the late 1970s, I stumbled into a small firestorm when I referred to Ontario as "a region." For a Western Canadian or an Atlantic Canadian, it is no bad thing to be called a "region." But Ontario members of my party sternly advised me that Ontario did not consider itself to be a region like the others. It took the national interest, and did not appreciate the implication that it had any smaller motive. In fact, for a long time, Ontario did believe that what was good for Canada was good for Ontario, and, on constitutional questions, if not always on others, successive leaders of Ontario were prepared to take large risks in what they saw as the national interest.

That attitude led John Robarts to convene the Confederation for Tomorrow Conference in 1967, when the country seemed to be sliding towards division. It led David Peterson to propose, during the Meech Lake discussion, compromises which no other province could afford to offer. It led Bob Rae to participate personally in the time-consuming ministerial negotiations in 1991, and caused his opposition parties, by and large, to support him.

It is interesting to note the public reaction to their initiatives. Mr. Robarts was universally praised, but Premiers Peterson and Rae had more difficulty, because the set of challenges which suddenly faced Canada as a whole was also shaking up Ontario. Prosperity, which had almost seemed a birthright, at least of Southern Ontario, was faltering there, as it had in other parts of Canada. Factories were closing, jobs were harder to find, communities which had taken their future for granted began to have doubts. The province was changing, and one result was that the wellsprings of Ontario generosity were being tested. More than other Canadians would comfortably admit, we have counted on Ontario to put the national interest first, and that will not be so automatic now. Circumstances have forced Ontario to become more like other provinces, more conscious of its own problems and interests and requirements.

Against that trend, which is primarily economic in its origin, there remains a powerful determination in Ontario to be part of a large and modern nation. Of all the Canadian provinces, Ontario, seems to me to be the least likely to be prepared to settle for some smaller arrangement, whether that is a diminished Canada or some kind of subsidiary affiliation with the United States. Ontario does not think small. In every field, from the arts to sport to business, it is a Big League province. Of course, the danger with Ontario is that, faced with what seemed to be an inevitable break-up in Canada, those instincts could lead to a quick embrace of the United States. Yet Ontario is also the home, virtually the citadel, of Canada's cultural nationalists. The challenge is to mobilize and combine those energies, of nationalism and ambition, to renew the remarkable country that we have.

But that will require more than a "quiet sense of ourselves." The attitudes in Canada, towards Canada, are much more complex today than they have ever been before.

Obviously, the actions of governments will influence those attitudes, for good or ill, in both Quebec and the rest of Canada. Prime Minister Chrétien has argued consistently, in his campaign and in government, that Canadians are tired of the constitution, and want action on tangible issues. He has directed his ministers to issues on which practical progress can be made – for example, barriers to interprovincial trade – and, for the moment, does not intend to undertake the development of new constitutional initiatives. That is a sensible way to start, although, as events unfold over the next year, Prime Minister Chrétien may decide that such initiatives are necessary.

But, under current circumstances, where time is limited and the real issue is as much attitude as jurisdiction, the actions of Canadian citizens will count as much as those of governments.

One of our mistakes in Canada is that we often underestimate the influence and the will of individual citizens. The juggernaut of television and polling and interest groups has led to a sense that individuals count for less than they did before. That may be true in some societies, or on some issues. But, in Canada, on the issue of our future as a country, individual attitudes and actions can make the difference.

Despite our immense geography, this is a very personal country, in which links of family and affiliation and experience connect us closely. I am amazed at the thousands of Canadians who, over my years in public life, stopped me to talk about their High River connection – a father who became a pilot at our Emergency Flying Training School, a grandfather who came west from P.E.I. on a threshing crew, a second cousin who was a Mountie or a roughneck or a student in my mother's school. Every Canadian community has similar stories, of personal and professional connections that matter to people.

Obviously, those links are less developed between Canadians in Quebec and those outside, and between individuals and groups who have been here some time and Canadians who have arrived more recently. But our national links cross even those differences – service clubs that operate in different provinces and languages, groups with similar social goals, farm organizations, women's groups, youth exchanges, hockey tournaments, churches.

For all those connections, we know very little about our extraordinary country, and are uncomfortable with the symbols or myths that would help us see ourselves as one community. Can we change that in time? This book is based on the premise that we can, if we try.

FIVE

IS THERE REALLY A CRISIS?

WHEN THE FIRST CHINESE IMMIGRANTS CAME TO THE SHORES OF this country, they called it the "Golden Mountain."

In Polish, "Canada" is the word for "good luck."

Martin Luther King recorded the codeword slaves used as they sought freedom here on our Underground Railroad. That word was "Heaven."

Those are flattering assessments of our country. And they are powerful – they have drawn millions of people to our shores, and nourished a comfortable sense of accomplishment, even superiority, at home.

Yet there is a trap in those assessments. They are about the physical Canada – the land, not the nation. They celebrate the space, the wealth, the sense of physical freedom and opportunity.

When you think about it, those physical qualities share two characteristics. First, we Canadians had little to do with them;

they were inherited, not formed. Second, they appear immutable, as though they will go on forever, despite us, not because of us. There will always be space in Canada, and wealth, and the freedom to lose one's self, or make one's self. So we are celebrated for what we have inherited, not for what we have done.

Other countries, with whom we compare ourselves, are assessed on different grounds. The United States is seen – by strangers as by citizens – as not just a land mass, but also an experiment and a power. The successful countries of Europe, and of Asia, are not just geographies, but also cultures, histories, societies.

Moreover, that one-dimensional celebration of the physical is unfair to Canada. Beyond the beauty of our land, we are also a unique and successful community.

Our own experiments have worked remarkably well, and we should celebrate them as well. For example, while we have tensions in our federal system now, we have, for 127 years, been remarkably successful in operating one of the most complex forms of government in the world. By their nature, federal systems are more difficult to sustain effectively than are smaller states with only one level of government and a homogeneous population. As a simple exercise in government, a Japan is much simpler to run than a Canada. Yet, judged by the results, we have managed our federalism very well, bringing and keeping together a scattered and highly diverse population, in an immense land mass, and building one of the strongest economies in the world and a model network of social policies.

We developed a strong and effective mixed economy, in which private-sector growth was encouraged, but the state was prepared to undertake large ventures – like a national broadcasting network, a national airline, and the Canadian Wheat

Board – which were too big for the private sector to handle at the time. Despite the controversy, our commitment to serving Canadians in two official languages works well. Our social programs have established a high standard of justice and security, and Canadian medicare is the model many Americans would adapt for use in their own society. We were the primary force in inventing the concept of international peacekeeping, and then members of the Canadian Armed Forces made that system work in troubled regions around the world.

And those Canadian successes were achieved on hard terrain. We settled the winter half of North America – driving rails through mountains, uniting vast and different territories, fighting the weather, embracing different cultures, and doing all that peacefully, by agreement not by conquest. Our land and space are essential to our character, but Canada is much more than a Golden Mountain.

And yet our image is physical, and we discount, or disdain, the political qualities which transformed the geography into a community, the land into a country. That threatens our future in two ways. The most obvious is that we don't remind ourselves enough about the way Canada came into being – about the courage and the compromise and the vision and the regrets of Macdonald or Laurier or Crowfoot or Riel or Agnes Macphail or Joe Howe or Henry Wise Wood or René Lévesque or the countless other figures whose stories, in other societies, would be the stuff of myth and learning. We don't know our own history, so we act as though we have none, as though we are simply campers here, on this Golden Mountain, protected by our great natural good fortune.

In ignoring our past we are left with the illusion that our future is inevitable, and that our country will stand or fall, like a tree in the forest, by natural forces. In fact, very little about Canada has been inevitable. We are a country built by will, often against nature. The most striking example was the railway. William Van Horne and his associates in that audacious venture decided to build their rail line through the Rocky Mountains a full year before the discovery of the Rogers Pass, which would make it possible. That was an extraordinary combination of daring and determination and, when it was done, Van Horne gave up his American citizenship, saying: "Building that railroad would have made a Canadian out of the German emperor." The railway is easier to visualize, because of the graphic image of rails reaching through those daunting mountains. Yet the same kind of will and imagination were needed to bring colonies together to create a country in Confederation, and to launch the national initiatives that became the Wheat Board, the Canadian Broadcasting Corporation, the Canada Council.

And if great daring was required to launch those Canadian initiatives, great care and sensitivity were needed to make them work. Certainly, the arrangements among governments in Canada have always been managed carefully, directed deliberately, sometimes to achieve unique arrangements, such as equalization, often simply to avoid a rending conflict.

We have been blessed by natural advantages, but that has not diminished the need to manage our complex country very carefully, and, over time, we have devised a series of programs and assumptions that made the most of our natural advantages. We were never a laissez-faire country, which simply followed the flow of events. We have been proactive – building the railway, the Seaway, the Roads to Resources; establishing a national airline, and then, after the Massey Commission, a national cultural policy; creating the system of equalization for poorer provinces, and a network of social policies which sought the same security for citizens that equalization gave provinces. One explanation of our success is that we have not left much to chance.

By the same token, one explanation of our current tensions is that our most basic assumptions no longer fit the country that we have become. For the sake of argument, consider four assumptions which have helped shape national policy in Canada since the Second World War. First, the nature of the international economy, and our inherent strengths, would combine to guarantee increasing prosperity for Canadians. Second, that prosperity would allow generous, even innovative, programs at home, for as far as the eye could see. Third, Ontario's dynamic growth and broad vision would provide sure and steady leadership for the country. And fourth, other Canadians would continue to welcome the leadership of what, in Halifax, is called, "Central Canada"; I have come to believe that is more than just a geographic term, and is also a wry Atlantic commentary on where power is seen to lie in the country. And that says nothing of other "status quo" assumptions, for example, that aboriginal people would continue to slip quietly into the dark margins of our society, or that immigration, or modern times, would leave our traditional communities intact.

The point is that none of those central assumptions applies in the Canada of 1994. The wrenching debate on the Free Trade Agreement forced us to begin to face international economic realities, where Canada can take nothing for granted. The burden of our debt has transformed the public agenda, forcing us to supplant the good things we want to do, with the harsh things we can't avoid. Ontario is not able to carry the rest of the country as much as it did in the past. And Quebec, and

Alberta, to name two, will not want a much larger role in defining the national future, in any event.

Against that background, I am surprised by the number of thoughtful Canadians, particularly outside Quebec, who assume that Canada will stay together in the future simply because it has stayed together in the past. I think those rose-coloured glasses are wrong in both lenses – naïvely distorting the roots and reasons for separatism in Quebec and the frustration in other parts of Canada.

Regarding Quebec, there still seems to be some belief that the leaders of Quebec are bluffing, trying to get more than their share from Confederation, and that, in the final analysis, the people of Quebec would not vote to leave. Other Canadians seem quite prepared to accept changes which would make Quebec more comfortable in Canada, but regard those changes as more a courtesy than a requirement. Still others seem to think that separation, if it came, would be relatively painless, just another manageable misfortune in a life that is sometimes up and sometimes down.

I think that blithe optimism reflects a serious misjudgement, both of attitudes in contemporary Quebec and of the reaction of the rest of Canada to a proposal of separation. What is more curious, even ironic, is that it accepts the conventional wisdom that the only real Canadian problem relates to Quebec. That is precisely the assumption which has guided policy-makers in Ottawa, and other capitals, for years – an assumption to which large numbers of Canadians, outside Quebec, objected in their rejection of the Meech Lake Accord.

My own view is that the momentum of separatism is a symptom of a more basic Canadian problem. We are like a wealthy middle-class family, successful by all the conventional standards, but lacking any real sense of purpose, and becoming more uncomfortable with one another. The result is that the demands, and the differences, of our individual members become more important than what we might do together. I try not to simplify separatism, but am convinced that part of what makes it so tempting is that Quebecers can find a purpose and vitality in the idea of an independent Quebec that they cannot find in the prospect of a united Canada.

And in reaching for a sense of purpose, Quebecers are not alone. The real issue for Canada is not the arrangements that would bring us together, but the reasons for making them. Simple unity is not an adequate national purpose, and that is particularly true if it seems to be achieved in the interest of only one community, while ignoring the interests of others.

The reality is that the "status quo" has few supporters in modern Canada. That is why British Columbians tune out of Canadian debates, and place more value on their relations with Asia, or with the U.S. Pacific Northwest. It is at the root of the anger that has become so evident in Alberta, but is laced through large parts of the country. It helps explain the growth of special-interest groups, whose appeal naturally intensifies if the larger interest seems irrelevant or remote. It is one reason we are so susceptible to the pull of U.S. culture. Canadians want change as well as unity.

SIX

"I Don't Want to Hear about the Constitution"

Public life has become extremely public in Canada. In earlier times, Mrs. St. Laurent, a poker player, could summon foreign service officers to leave work and play a few hands in the prime minister's residence, and not a word appeared in the media. Today there would be photographs of the players leaving their desks, speculation on what vital Canadian interests were imperilled by their absence, and an Access to Information submission demanding to know who paid for the deck of cards.

Today, being in public office means that your slightest misadventure becomes national news.

That, by the way, is why photographers and television crews used to cluster, in the Centre Block of Parliament, at the bottom of the stairway which ministers took to enter the House of Commons. The pictures they took, day after day, were about as exciting as coverage of traffic crossing the Lions Gate Bridge.

But there was always the chance that a minister would stumble on those slippery stone steps – and then there would be a photo seen round the world.

That is part of modern "gotcha" journalism, and Maureen and I encountered a milder version when we hosted our first garden party at Stornoway – the official residence in Ottawa of the Leader of Her Majesty's Loyal Opposition.

The party attracted some uninvited guests – a family of skunks, who were minding their own business deep under our porch. No one provoked them, but the day was humid, and you knew they were there. Charles Lynch dutifully recorded their presence in his Southam's column from Ottawa.

So the graphic phrase "as popular as a skunk at a garden party" has stayed in my mind. I think it applies to current Canadian attitudes towards constitutional talks.

No one wants them now and, indeed, our experience has been so frustrating that no one really wants to contemplate them for the future. The failure of the Meech Lake process and the Charlottetown referendum have made it very difficult to go back, one more time, to try again. The country has no tolerance for new constitutional initiatives, and no one understands that better than I do.

But the problems those earlier initiatives sought to resolve have not gone away. It is simply useless to pretend that Quebecers would vote in a referendum for a "status-quo Canada," or that the anger and anguish among aboriginals could be contained by a royal commission study, or that the rejection of the Charlottetown Senate proposals will end the debate about institutional reform.

In fact, a period when nothing was done on constitutional questions would be quite an extraordinary break with history.

We have often had the good sense to call them something else, but there have always been constitutional negotiations in Canada. That is how the country came to exist. Other nations fought their way onto the world's map by revolution or by winning or losing a war. We are a nation by agreement. That is how we started, how we function, how we succeed or fail.

One of the reasons Canada has succeeded, as a federation and as a national community, has been our ability to adapt. When new provinces entered Confederation, new arrangements were made, and Confederation changed. Newfoundland, for example, required specific references to its denominational schools. The simple addition of new provinces changed the balance between Quebec and the provinces whose principal language was English. Alberta and Saskatchewan did not exercise the full powers of other provinces for nearly thirty years after they acquired provincehood. The Yukon and Northwest territories are gradually exercising powers of self-government that bring them closer, year by year, to full provincial status. The legislature of New Brunswick has deliberately established the bilingual status of that province. The federation changes regularly, adapting to new realities. When persistent economic disparity threatened Canadian standards, the system of equalization was introduced, to establish a basic equality of services for Canadians everywhere. New arrangements were made, and Confederation changed. And when Canadian society wanted pensions, or medicare, new arrangements were made and Confederation changed.

It may be that a new initiative now need not be "constitutional" in a formal sense. Our system has been quite successful in making pragmatic changes, one by one, relatively quickly. Certainly there is an option of making administrative arrangements – deals among governments – whose effect would be to resolve individual important issues. That was done when an agreement was signed between the federal government and Quebec, giving that province a larger role in Canadian decisions respecting new immigrants who want to come to Quebec. It was done, in effect, when provinces were brought into the process of negotiating international trade agreements, even though, strictly speaking, that is an exclusive responsibility of the federal government. That path of administrative arrangements should be pursued, as far as it goes.

But it begs a basic question: is the Canadian problem that the details don't work, or that the system doesn't work?

Quiet administrative changes can take care of details, including significant ones. But if we are to make changes to the system itself – changes, for example, which might yield real reform of the Senate, or the formal recognition of the "distinct society" of Quebec or of the inherent aboriginal right to self-government in Canada – we cannot do that by administrative arrangements.

Moreover, we cannot do it quietly and, in my view, should not try. Because part of what is transforming Canada (and other Western societies) is the inexorable reality that a more educated, more informed citizenry insists on taking a larger role in public decisions.

Constitution-making is more political than legal. Laws are the consequence, but political agreement is what counts. I do not disparage the complexity or importance of the traditional legal questions of constitutional principle and practice. Constitutional decisions end up as laws, or as matters for the courts. But the issues are political.

The nation needs to come to judgements on the role of Quebec in Canada, the role of aboriginals, the influence of the West, the status of women, the shape and nature of our institutions. Those are all political questions, in the best sense of that phrase. They have to do with our political community: how we live together, how we treat one another, who we are. Issues like that cannot be resolved by administrative arrangements.

During the Charlottetown process, virtually everyone said we should settle the constitution so we could get on to the really important questions facing Canada. I do not think many of those voices were saying that, for example, the future of Quebec or the status of aboriginals was unimportant. Instead, they were frustrated by the way those issues were being addressed. If the constitutional questions are, by definition, political, so is the process of constitutional discussion. It may be that the abiding frustration of Canadians is not with the issues themselves, but with a process that often seemed to confirm the worst caricatures of politics.

So the question becomes whether those "constitutional" issues are urgent for Canada now.

My own view is that the questions relating to Quebec *are* urgent. There will very likely be another referendum soon in Quebec. If there is no tangible change in the constitutional status quo, the rest of Canada is virtually inviting Quebec to vote to leave.

The aboriginal and institutional issues, if less urgent, are nonetheless important enough that it is hard to contemplate a constitutional agreement that affects Quebec alone.

So, as a practical matter, we cannot walk away from the major political issues which have been at the heart of the failed formal attempts at constitutional reform. We can't treat the constitution as if it is a skunk at our party. The absence of a new initiative could mean the failure of the country – and I believe very few Canadians want that.

The basic attitude in Quebec towards Canada is not clear,

in part because Quebecers are being offered the beguiling alternative of independence. But I believe the separatists are gaining by default, and that many Quebecers are being driven to that alternative because it has been so difficult to change the status quo, and the failures of the attempts to change it have created an impression that Quebec is not wanted in the larger country. Quebecers have been driven to the devil they do not know. However seductive the alternative of independence, everything I know tells me the great majority of Quebecers would prefer a Canada that clearly wanted them.

And certainly, no other part of the country is proposing to separate. Some Western Canadians are prepared to contemplate the separation of Quebec, rather than acquiesce in changes they consider unwarranted, but very few actively propose an end to the country. Most Canadians want Canada to reform itself, but to continue.

Rather than lose the country by default, it behooves us to make two inquiries. Why did the formal constitutional initiatives fail? And, given the fatigue with formal initiatives, what can be done to let Canadians reform a country they want to keep?

SEVEN

REACHING OVER DIFFERENCES

IN TIME, THERE WILL HAVE TO BE NEW FORMAL NEGOTIATIONS directed either to dividing the country or to reforming it, because the status quo won't work. In fact, I believe that, if we are serious about resisting separatism, we must assure potential separatists that there will be constitutional change. In order for that process to work, the negotiation will have to be something like a Canada Round, with a broad agenda.

But that is for later, not for now. What is needed now is to understand what the problems are, and why Canadians, instead of looking for agreement, seem to want to disagree.

One of my first public meetings, as Constitutional Affairs minister, was in the city council chambers in Yellowknife. During the conversation, Pat McMahon, the mayor of Yellowknife, said: "In Canada, everyone feels misunderstood." She's right, and one result is that virtually everyone sees the country through his or her particular lens, which distorts the whole by making the viewer's preoccupations seem larger than life, and those of others seem smaller.

Another result is that everyone insists on his or her view being understood, before trying to understand the views of others.

Both those attitudes were abundantly evident during the Charlottetown process. The most thoughtful Quebecers were so focused on their own concerns that they could not treat seriously the Western Canadian and Newfoundland preoccupation with Senate reform. To Quebecers, the Senate was an issue of a different order, an inferior order, from the questions that they believed to be at the heart of the constitution.

For their part, many Western Canadian leaders seemed genuinely to believe that threats of independence in Quebec were a bluff – one that it would be better not to call, but a bluff nonetheless.

For their part, aboriginal leaders saw their own issues as the compelling priority.

In no case was this narrow and exclusive focus a tactic. It reflected a deep and genuine difference of opinion over what the issues were, and what the priorities should be. And the different perspectives in the negotiating room reflected even more profound differences in the country.

What is encouraging is that the Charlottetown process reached over those differences. The seventeen delegations came to a unanimous agreement that took account of everyone's priorities. In the case of Meech Lake, there had been complaints of unfair pressure, leaving the impression that the Meech agreement was forced and artificial. There were no such complaints about the Charlottetown Accord. Individual participants might have preferred different details, but none claimed his hand was forced.

The referendum was a different story. Something happened around those negotiating tables that didn't happen in the country. What was it?

I think there were three factors.

First, the people at the tables were in the business of getting agreement, settling disputes. That is both their personal disposition and their public responsibility. They are all leaders of large and diverse communities and, however strong their own preference or prejudice, know they have to accommodate others. That is as much the case for an aboriginal leader as for anyone else who holds high public office.

Second, they all came to believe that the issues were important, and could not go unresolved forever. So they had a sense of deadline, as well as a disposition to agree.

Third, they were face to face with other Canadians who often had a different view of the country we share, and they all learned from one another. That was the critical factor. Being in the room together taught us things we could not have learned at long distance. Often what was learned was intangible: how genuinely the poorer parts of Canada depend upon the knowledge that the larger Canada is there to offer help when they need it; how thoroughly aboriginal leaders believe the larger country will let them down; how unrelated to everyday reality in British Columbia are the questions which drive the traditional constitutional debate in Canada; how much generosity there is when Canadians come to understand one another's differences; and how much ingenuity can result once goodwill is established and problems are treated as solvable, not insurmountable. What is important is that those lessons were not just about individuals in the room. By definition, and in fact, those individuals represented larger forces in the country, forces often removed from one another, and suspicious or insensitive as a result. So it is reasonable to believe that the understanding, and generosity, that emerged in the room could emerge in the country, if we could find a way to bring Canadians together, face to face.

The National Film Board had asked that they be allowed to bring cameras and microphones into the negotiation process, so there could be a graphic and reliable record of an undertaking that might change Canadian history. I refused the request, because cameras create the expectation of an audience, and take away some of the spontaneity and frankness which I thought would be essential to any success. But I regret that there is no graphic and objective record because, when the agreements began to occur, the atmosphere was like nothing I have ever experienced before. The phrases are suspect, but it made you proud of your country, and proved clearly, to all the participants, that we Canadians belong together as one country. The irony is that, had the cameras been present, there might have been no history to record; yet, had there been a visual record of that genuine, human give-and-take, I believe that would have led Canadians to support the result.

Of course, in ventures of that kind, experience and expertise matter. But they are not the critical component. These are human and emotional challenges – any negotiation is, but particularly one about your country. What made the difference, time after time, was when one individual convinced another that it was right to consider a different approach. And, on one occasion or another, all participants around those tables modified their opinion or approach. Sometimes that change was on substantive issues, and sometimes on practical ones. One afternoon in Edmonton, running late, after a frustrating discussion, I adjourned a meeting without calling on Rosemary Kuptana, president of the Inuit Tapirisat, who had just signalled an interest in speaking. It is a chairman's lot to cut off people who should be heard, and we were all late for some other engagement. As I was gathering my papers, Rosemary came to me, smiled, and said: "A little courtesy would go a long way." There was no point of order, and no press conference, but her gentle reprimand affected every subsequent meeting I chaired, and helped create an atmosphere where agreement became possible.

The people ranged around those negotiating tables were not easy-going personalities, and many of them were bruised by earlier encounters. Nonetheless, Rosemary Kuptana's courtesy proved contagious, and people listened intently to others, and came finally to trust and respect them, and we found common ground. That is the way public policy is supposed to be made and, despite substantial differences – of perspective and of personality – the process worked.

That is critically important now, because public-policy decisions are moving out from the leaders to the public. That is not the result of devices like a referendum but, in effect, the result of the success of democratic societies in providing a broader base of education and information, and inculcating a greater sense of efficacy.

There was a time when the views of the Canadians outside the negotiating rooms didn't matter much. There was a sharper division of responsibility between leaders and citizens. So-called ordinary Canadians did not consider themselves particularly informed about constitutional issues and, more generally, were more disposed to let their leaders make decisions.

That deference to leaders has been changing steadily. On issues like the environment, "citizen opinion" has become a regular, and often decisive, part of the equation. That has been less the case on other issues, including constitutional ones.

In fact, the traditional practice was to regard federal-provincial, and constitutional, discussions as the preserve of heads of government, and of executive federalism, without much regard to Parliament and legislatures, let alone the public. That changed suddenly, in English-speaking Canada, with the Meech Lake Accord.

The only thing different about the Meech Lake process was the opposition it inspired. The particulars were those used in every significant federal-provincial discussion in Canadian history, including the Confederation agreements – closed meetings, selective agendas, bargaining, and not-so-subtle pressure. However, that was one of the reasons why the Meech Lake negotiation was so traumatic for its participants: it was one of those flashpoints where old practices collide with new expectations.

From now on, questions about arrangements for the future of Canada will be public, for the living room, not just the negotiating room. If we want agreement on solutions, we need agreement on what the problems are. An atmosphere in which "everyone feels misunderstood" won't help.

If this were a postage stamp of a country, we could simply bring people together, face to face, as we did successfully with the leaders in the Charlottetown process. But this is the second-largest country in the world – distant, different, difficult. We need to establish the context of a common purpose before we can get the detailed agreements we seek.

The challenge now is not simply to find arrangements that will work. That was done at Charlottetown. It is to find arrangements that will both work and be accepted. And that means we must pay far more attention than we have to helping Canadians understand their country.

It is a commonplace in Canada that most of us don't know

much about Canadians in other regions. We sometimes watch the news, and have a sense of life as it is lived in the headlines in other provinces, but not much real sense of where people work, how they relax, what they think, and why they think it.

Travel is expensive, and the winters are long, so most Canadians stay in their own region, or cut south to the sunshine. How can Quebecers who holiday in Vermont or Florida know anything about Alberta? How can Albertans who holiday in Montana or Hawaii know anything about Quebec?

We have very little personal experience of one another. Therefore, we rely upon our schools, our media, our national institutions to help us understand our fellow citizens. Some schools, some teachers, make extraordinary efforts. Some media, like Peter Gzowski's programs and occasional print journalism, bring their audiences inside the life of other Canadians. Some initiatives of national institutions – whether "Canada 125" travel for young Canadians, or the Bronfman *Heritage Minutes*, or the Rotary "Adventures in Citizenship" – change the lives of the Canadians they touch. But those are the exceptions, and even they touch only a small proportion of our population.

Two other factors complicate the problem. The United States, our omnipresent neighbour and inescapable exemplar, overcomes similar problems by a mix of patriotism and symbols which we find, alternatively, hard to take and hard to imitate. We have become more self-conscious about our national symbols recently – flying the flag more, trying to learn the words to the national anthem, even having school choirs sing that anthem in both our official languages – but national myths don't come as naturally to us as to our neighbours.

For example, Quebec was not much impressed by the

symbolic patriation of our constitution, home from Britain, in 1982, because it was accompanied by constitutional amendments which Quebec found offensive.

In February 1994, at the University of Calgary, a bright young graduate student, who comes from Red Deer, reminded me that the maple tree, from which comes the leaf that symbolizes Canada, doesn't grow in Alberta. It is not unusual for Canadians to see national symbols through a very local prism, and find them wanting.

The other factor, becoming more serious, is that much of our information about other Canadians is wrong. Will Rogers might have had Canada in mind, years ago, when he said: "It's not what we don't know that is the problem. It's what we know that ain't so." Sometimes that is simple ignorance, based innocently on false impressions.

That was the case, for example, with a group of Quebec journalists who accepted an invitation from the Calgary Chamber of Commerce and the Stampede Board to visit Alberta for Stampede Week in 1991. Their trip took them down to the Crows Nest Pass, in southwestern Alberta, then up a magnificent highway where the foothills meet the mountains, through Alberta ranch country. They didn't meet many French-speakers along that route so, when Maureen and I met them at the O-H Ranch in Longview, they burst forth in enthusiasm about the scenery and hospitality and surprises they had found. One surprise was that they had not known how vast the ranches were in Alberta. The television footage they had seen, in Quebec, about my province focused on oil rigs and cities, and that formed their image of a province where there had been ranches before there were cities, and long before the discovery of oil. I wondered what else about Alberta, things that I took for granted, they did not know; and what essential truths about Quebec would not be known by the Albertans they visited.

Ideally, all Canadians should know much more about how our country came to be, and how its different citizens and communities see themselves. Simply focusing on that goal — treating it as important — would help Canadians understand their country. But it is too late for a crash course in Canadian history. And, in any event, our present challenge is much more modest. It is not to know Canada perfectly, but simply to have a realistic basis for assessing why the country is at risk today, and whether it is worth keeping. A decision on the future of a country like Canada should be as rational as possible, based upon some common understanding of what the problems are.

I am not a historian in any academic sense. Most of what I know about our country came firsthand, in the honourable profession of politics, working with Canadians, community by community, often crisis by crisis, learning to see my country as others saw it.

I have been very lucky, both in coming from a part of Alberta that has a palpable sense of its own identity and worth, and in my opportunities in public life.

Hollywood has created a John Wayne myth about Western towns, and perhaps that image of the solitary figure casting a long male shadow over the empty plain fits in Texas or Oklahoma. But it was as distant as the moon from my life in High River, where the ranchers and farmers and tradespeople built churches and community halls, and a society where people could call upon, and count upon, one another.

The particular culture of High River was influenced by British settlers, who brought as much of England as they could to their rough ranches in the foothills. But the basic sense of community was native to the place, and to the experience. It was in the nature of people building new futures in uncertain terrain. You were disposed to be interested in your neighbours.

Then, at age thirty-six, I became the leader of a national party. It was clear that neither my natural charisma nor my experience would sweep us into office. Large parts of the country knew nothing of me, and were suspicious of my party. That was particularly true in Quebec, despite the real respect which my predecessor, the Right Honourable Robert Stanfield, had won personally. So I spent much of the next three years on the road in Canada, asking as many questions as I answered, trying to convert the distrust of the Trudeau government into positive support for an alternative.

However effective that was as election strategy, it was a wonderful education, not only about the different parts of Canada, but about how they relate, or might relate, to each other. I was on that road as the leader of a national party, needing to understand local interests, and looking for ways to make them fit in to the larger interest of the country. That was not simply my disposition. It was the attitude of most of my party, including the MPs who had first come into Parliament in 1972. We had all been shaped by Mr. Stanfield's observation that it was always easy in Canada to unite most of the country against part of the country, but that a genuinely national party, by definition, could not do that.

When I was thrust back into Canadian domestic issues, in 1991, as minister of Constitutional Affairs, I went on the road again. My daughter, Catherine, best characterized the change, on the day I was "sworn out" of External Affairs and "sworn in" to my new portfolio. "Well," she said, "so long Paris, hello Moose Jaw." In fact, I didn't make Moose Jaw on this pilgrimage. But

I was in Estevan and Valleyfield and Kentville and Iqualuit and Squamish and Niagara-on-the-Lake and a hundred other Canadian communities, immersed again in my country. Obviously, circumstances had changed in the intervening fifteen years.

Lines were more sharply drawn. The public distrust, which had focused earlier on individuals in politics, had extended to a general cynicism about the political system. Quebecers were profoundly tired of the endless debate about their future. More Western Canadians had become more aggressive in insisting that their concerns must be addressed too. Aboriginal issues seemed more urgent. Tempers were shorter, and there was more willingness to treat other Canadians as adversaries.

But the basic realities were the same. The basic interests of different people and regions and communities had not changed, and were not in any fundamental conflict. To declare a country a failure, you must conclude that there are irreconcilable differences, that its parts cannot work together. That was not the country I found, in either the late 1970s or the early 1990s.

Indeed, I believe the differing Canadian interests can work together easily, if we can clear away some serious misunderstandings which are intensely held, and if we can come to focus on the compelling interests which we have in common. I believe the problem is not in what we are, but in how we see one another.

As a step towards some consensus on our interests and our disagreements, I am setting forth what I have learned of current attitudes in each of the West, the aboriginal community, and Quebec. I don't pretend that those are the only communities that seek changes in Canada. But they represent the principal forces which must be reconciled if we are to function as a whole community, able to respond to other challenges.

EIGHT

THE WEST

LET ME START AT HOME, NOT JUST BECAUSE THE WEST IS WHERE I come from, but also because, habitually, the discomfort of the West within Canada has been discounted as being less justified, or less important, than the concerns of Quebec or of the aboriginal peoples. There is no sure scale on which to weigh grievance, but that very habit of discounting Western Canada's concerns has intensified the sense of alienation, particularly in Alberta and British Columbia, the two Western provinces with power, the two provinces which, economically and psychologically, can afford to get angry.

At the heart of that anger is precisely the conviction that, when the "Canadian national interest" is defined, the West is not taken seriously.

That conviction is as old as the region. Ask Louis Riel. Ask the farmers who fought the tariff. Ask the businesses denied credit by "Eastern" banks.

What is new is a sense of power, a sense that the West is strong enough now that it doesn't have to put up with being put down.

There are, of course, different Wests and different Westerners. On specific questions, those differences are sharp. In my own province, on questions like gun control or the environment or Quebec, where the caricature has Albertans speaking with one dyspeptic voice, there is in fact a wide range of views. The same is true in every province, and in the Territories.

And it is true among provincial governments. For example, when the question is: "How strong should the central government be in Canada?", the governments of Saskatchewan and Manitoba, which depend more on national programs and transfer payments, generally opt for more strength at the centre, and the governments of Alberta and British Columbia generally opt to decentralize Ottawa's power. That is not a party matter; in the most recent negotiations, B.C. New Democrats and Alberta Conservatives were on one side of the argument, and Saskatchewan New Democrats and Manitoba Conservatives on the other.

But, with all those differences, a generalization applies: Western Canada, as a region, does not feel as much a part of Canada as the Atlantic provinces do, or Ontario, or even Quebec. That sense of being "outside" has deep roots, and it has become intensified in the last fifteen years.

Of course, there is a certain cachet to being an "outsider." That is an identity in itself, and often provides comforting explanations of any misadventure, from not knowing which fork to use to not getting the loan. So it is easy to dismiss an "outsider" feeling as an excuse or escape. But, to speak personally, the sense of being an "outsider" in Canada just came with my territory. That is what we were, even in the most comfortable precincts of Alberta.

I was very lucky growing up in a family where both parents worked at jobs they enjoyed, there was food on the table, the banks didn't foreclose, the roof didn't leak. No one could write a country-and-western song about us – or, for that matter, about our country-and-western town. There were places in Alberta where the mines closed, or there were fires or disasters, or the community wasted away to a ghost town. But that was not our story. High River had its share of personal tragedy, but it was both a successful and an optimistic town, not a nest for grievance.

Moreover, there were ample connections with the rest of Canada. The Blakes and the Farquharsons were from Prince Edward Island; the first large general store had been built and operated by Joseph Limoges, in whose home French was the first language; there were Nova Scotians, New Brunswickers, and countless families who had come from Ontario, or moved through or from the Prairies and the American West. We were not back of beyond.

Yet, even in that comfortable setting, you grew up knowing that you were out on the edge, not at the centre. In one sense, that is a challenging place to be, maybe a better place than at the centre of constraining pressures and traditions. But you knew that the centre had a hold on you, and that the relation was unequal.

To the degree you thought about Canadian institutions, they were all somewhere else – Parliament, the CBC, the banks, the Toronto Maple Leafs, the Montreal Canadiens, the "great universities" were all in the East. So, if you thought about it, was power. The West contributed folklore – "Jake and the Kid," the Indians and their feathers, the Calgarians riding horses into the Royal York Hotel at Grey Cup, the "men in sheepskin coats," the odd earnest politicians who popped in from the West with their eccentric nostrums.

For a time, no one made much of an issue of the West being "outside." That was a reality too self-evident to need underlining. The 1940s and 1950s were defined in Alberta by, consecutively, the war, the return of servicemen, the great oil discovery at Leduc. People became self-absorbed and relatively prosperous.

But a harsher memory hung in the air. The Depression hurt everywhere, but devastated the prairie West, literally blowing away homes and hopes, and making concrete the sense that the people in power in Canada would not be much help. That was when William Aberhart railed against the "fifty big shots," the Eastern banks, the Eastern press. The seeds were sewn that became the CCF and, later, the NDP. R.B. Bennett, the Calgary Conservative prime minister, became memorialized by the "Bennett buggy," the automobile you couldn't afford to drive, so hitched to horses.

If there was any natural momentum for integrating the West into the country, it was dissipated by the Depression, which was both an economic and a political experience in the West. It became part of the collective memory of those who grew up in the more tranquil 1940s and 1950s, marking the West as a place apart from the rest of the country.

One comment symbolized that for me. The Alberta Progressive Conservative party had elected a grand total of one member to the Alberta Legislature in the general election of 1959. He was Ernest Watkins, a Calgary lawyer and BBC broadcaster who had emigrated to Canada – a "Canadian by choice," an Albertan by choice, and a man who usually took a large view of events. I was among a group of university student volunteers who helped him prepare for his lonely responsibilities in the legislature, and I regarded him as among my mentors.

In 1960, I had applied for a summer job with Canadian Press in Toronto (to write Ontario obituaries). One April day, I was told I was hired and, by happenstance, met Ernest Watkins on an Edmonton street.

"Mr. Watkins," I exulted, "I just got a summer job in Toronto." To which he replied: "Why?"

It wasn't a joke. This worldly Calgarian really didn't understand why an active young Albertan would want to go off to the East, even for a summer (even to write Ontario obituaries).

Today, Alberta's attitude towards Canada is the most aggressive in the West. The attitude in British Columbia is more benign, because there is a growing assumption that British Columbia is in a world of its own: it trades more with Asia than with the United States; it is exploring regional arrangements with Washington, Oregon, and California; the society west of the Rocky Mountains has always considered itself different from the rest of Canada and, if anything, the ties built by Sir John A.'s railway mean less today than ever. That attitude is expressed aggressively by some in British Columbia, but the larger attitude is more passive, more serene, grounded in a sense that Canada is a different country from British Columbia.

There is no referendum campaign stirring ideas of independence on the West Coast, but, psychologically, I think that British Columbia is the province most separated from the rest of Canada. It has not been at the heart of the history of the country, as Quebec has been for centuries, so the connecting roots are not as deep, nor as strong. Nor is there much sense that Confederation brings tangible benefits; the province simply assumes that B.C.'s interests are an afterthought when "national policy" is decided, whether that is on Parliament Hill or on Bay Street.

That is not to deny the Canadian pride and patriotism of many individual British Columbians, nor to say there is an animosity towards the rest of Canada. That would almost be easier to address. Instead, there is not much interest in the larger country, not much sense of connection or of relevance. That stark ridge of Rocky Mountains is much more than a symbolic barrier. It is a line of real demarcation. The climate is different, and so are the economy, the lifestyle, the range of issues that engages the public.

To my mind, it is not a question of "holding" British Columbia in Canada, but one of reversing its steady drift away, and we cannot count on simple patriotism, or inertia. As a practical matter, there is a burden of proof on Canada, the need to demonstrate that we can become the kind of modern national community of which British Columbia, like Quebec, will want to be an active part.

Alberta, by contrast, will not drift away. Its instinct is to stay and fight, and Alberta's more aggressive attitude is worth analysing, because it will continue to set the agenda for much of the West. I think its roots are the following.

The West was not part of Confederation. That deal was made elsewhere, by others. Indeed, when Alberta and Saskatchewan came in, they were denied control of their own natural resources, even though other provinces were not so denied. There has always been a sense, first, that the Canadian system was imposed by someone else, and, second, that the West was powerless to do anything about that.

Certainly, the national political party system never established itself in Western Canada to the degree it did east of the Lakehead. Alberta occasionally sent Liberal or Progressive

Conservative MPs to Ottawa before 1957, from our cities, but the majority of MPs were from third parties, with scant influence on national affairs.

The same was largely true of Saskatchewan and Manitoba, except that the Saskatchewan regional party became the national CCF and NDP, and both Saskatchewan and Manitoba elected MPs, like Jimmy Gardiner and Stuart Garson, who became significant ministers in national Liberal governments.

Provincial governments in the three Prairie provinces were, by and large, formed by parties other than the two national parties. That lasted until the Diefenbaker elections, which were followed by the success of Progressive Conservative parties in Manitoba, Alberta, and Saskatchewan.

I think that electoral behaviour masked a larger reality. The prairie West was never really integrated into pan-Canadian systems, and neither the region nor the systems much cared. Occasionally, anger at a pan-Canadian system led to the establishment of a particular Western institution, as when Alberta, fed up with the banks, set up the Treasury Branch. But, generally, the West felt there was little it could do. And besides, after the Second World War, the region became more prosperous, with the discovery of oil and the postwar boom, and institutional arrangements didn't matter much. But the fact persisted that the West did not feel part of the country in the way that other regions did.

What changed was the sense of powerlessness. Mr. Diefenbaker's victory in 1957 was a watershed election for several reasons, breaking several old patterns. It led to the first votes for Indian people, to the nomination of Ellen Fairclough as the first woman in Cabinet in Canadian history, and to the Ukrainian-Canadian Michael Starr as the first minister whose origin was neither French nor Anglo-Saxon.

But it was also a Western victory and, if Mr. Diefenbaker was not in the end successful in being seen as a pan-Canadian leader, he was certainly always seen as a Western leader. He demonstrated that it was not impossible for a Westerner to succeed in national institutions, and make them more hospitable to the region that had been outside.

Another major change was economic. The economy of Alberta, in particular, became stronger, and more diversified. The energy industry was genuinely international, operating around the world, and both proud and self-conscious about being rooted in Calgary. When events in Quebec caused other businesses to begin to leak out of Montreal, several of them came to Calgary, and the city, and thus the province, began to see itself as a power in the world, and thus the Canadian, economy. That optimism created a great opportunity to connect the West and the country.

There is no point to regret, but certainly I am aware that, if my minority government had stayed in office in 1979, we would probably have been able to integrate the interests of the region and the country. Instead, the opposite happened.

The resurrected Trudeau government introduced the National Energy Program, which turned that latent optimism about being able to count in Canada into a profound sense of being victimized. It was the perfect proof of the suspicion that the national interest was aligned against the West; proof that the earlier optimism was misplaced; and a warning to be suspicious about measures coming out of Ottawa, disguised as the "national interest."

From that perspective, the Official Languages Act is seen as forcing French down Albertan throats, even though it doesn't. That was demonstrated during the 1988 federal election campaign in my constituency of Yellowhead, by an exchange that occurred at an all-candidates forum, in the town of Barrhead, between the Liberal party candidate, John Higgerty, and a voter who felt threatened by the Official Languages Act. Higgerty asked: "Is there one single person in this room who had to learn French to get your job, or has to learn it to keep your job? If so, please raise your hand." There were some 600 people in the room, and not a single hand went up. Then I raised mine, because learning French had certainly helped my career. But no one else in that room was directly affected by the Official Languages Act.

Higgerty had taken on the myth, and proven it false, but too often Canadians don't look behind the angry allegations, and false impressions acquire the force of fact. In the West, that can only deepen the sense of anger and alienation. The Official Languages Act has its faults, but the damning charge that it forces English-speaking Canadians to learn French is simply not true.

In an atmosphere so freighted with suspicion, the Meech Lake Accord was seen as another "Eastern" attempt to subordinate Western Canadian requirements for Senate reform, even though the decision to proceed with a "Quebec Round" first was taken, not in Ottawa or Quebec, but in Edmonton, unanimously, by the premiers. The scepticism about the Senate reform proposed later, in the Charlottetown Accord, compounded that suspicion and, gradually, the mood hardened in Alberta into an assumption that the national government and the West were marching to different drummers.

One dangerous twist in that mood concerned Quebec, explicitly. Despite the fierce conflict between Alberta and Ottawa over the National Energy Program, the Lougheed government was very careful to separate relations with Quebec from the fight with the Trudeau government. Indeed, on the question of natural resource jurisdiction, as on constitutional questions generally, Quebec and Alberta were allies. But the nature of the National Energy Program debate aroused basic antagonisms in Alberta, including antagonism to the province that was the *château fort* of the Trudeau government.

A theme emerged which, at its crudest, argued that the threat of independence was just a ploy used by Quebec to extract special treatment from any Ottawa government, and that the appropriate Alberta response was to "call Quebec's bluff" and find some Western way to blackmail Ottawa. That theme became a staple of Albertans whose attitude towards Quebec was unhindered by either knowledge or sympathy. But it took hold in the province, and is a significant factor today.

So that is the context in which the most recent Alberta demand for institutional change was fashioned. The basic premise has three elements: first, that the Canadian system is biased fundamentally against Western Canada; second, that bias can do fatal harm, witness the National Energy Program; and third, that the bias can be removed only by a change in the system, whose result is to give real power to the West.

The "Triple-E Senate" – "Elected, Effective, Equal" – became the instrument and symbol of that reform. Because that is the U.S. model, some critics interpreted the proposal as simply an "Americanization" embraced by the "most American" of Canada's regions. That trivializes the fundamental sense of exclusion which is a primary motive of a cross-section of people who set the political agenda in Alberta and, to a lesser extent, the West as a whole. That sense of exclusion must be overcome, and a legitimate means of integration must be found, if we are to build a Canada which can earn the loyalty of the West.

NINE

THE ABORIGINAL
COMMUNITY

HIGH RIVER WAS ORIGINALLY CALLED "SPITZEE," A BLACKFOOT
word which, I am told, translates roughly into "place where the
river is easy to cross." It lies along what we call the Highwood
River, at a point where the foothills flatten into prairie. It is a
beautiful place, with the Rocky Mountains looming to the west,
and the prairie stretching east, and, long before European settlement, Native tribes were drawn to the trees along that water.
Sometime in the last century, lightning struck a young poplar,
driving one of its limbs into an adjacent tree, where it germi-
nated. So the two trees grew together, on the river bank, linked
by a common limb. The Blackfoot named that "the Medicine
Tree," and gathered there for ceremonies. When the Medicine
Tree finally died and fell, that connecting limb was brought into
the town, and made the focal point of our community park.

That was one of the three ways in which, to my recollection,

High River acknowledged its "first people." We also made a point of recalling that the late W.E.G. Holmes was the "first white child" born in High River, thus setting a marker as to where our history started. And, whenever there was a rodeo or a ceremony, we invited Stoney and Blackfoot Indians to come in their costumes and head-dresses.

There was no intentional disrespect in those actions. On the contrary, to the degree anyone thought about it, High River judged its relations with the Native people to be good. In fact, there was little of the tension that existed in other Alberta towns, and I like to think that High River took some pride in that fact. But the reality was that we did not regard Native people as our equals, and, with the exception of some of our outdoorsmen, there was not much sense that we could learn from their lives and experience.

Particularly when I travelled internationally, and saw the conditions in which most of the world's children are raised, I was immensely grateful for my own good luck, growing up in Canada, in High River. Yet, had fortune placed me a few kilometres west, on the Stoney Reserve at Eden Valley, I would have had a very different future. And the difference, I have come to believe, relates principally to respect.

Yvon Dumont is now the lieutenant-governor of Manitoba, the first Métis to hold that office, in the province which Louis Riel formed. But before that, he led Métis delegations through two rounds of constitutional negotiations. One summer day, in 1991, at a festival in his home community of St. Laurent, he introduced me to some young Métis, just entering their teens. "At home," he said, "they are told there is one Métis hero, one of their people who made a great difference, and that is Louis Riel. And then they go to school and they are told that Canada, their country, regards their hero as a traitor."

In 1992, to their credit, the House of Commons and the Senate adopted unanimously a resolution recognizing "the unique and historic role of Louis Riel as a founder of Manitoba and his contribution in the development of Confederation." That will reduce one pressure on young Métis students, and it is doubly important because it is a deliberate act, by the whole Parliament, designed to demonstrate respect for aboriginal people.

But respect cannot be bestowed, or declared by Parliament. It exists, or it doesn't. For a long, long time, the larger Canadian community has not treated Canadian Indians or Inuit or Métis with respect. At our worst, we have regarded them as derelicts or hapless victims; at our best, we have honoured some of their claims and traditions. But, by and large, we have done even that on our terms, as a sort of gift from Canada, to the people who were here first.

The results have been tragic. Societies that were once self-reliant became dependent, and the social consequences are a source of shame to Canada.

Infant mortality among aboriginal Canadians is double the national average.

Suicide is twice as common.

The rate of tuberculosis is ten times higher.

The proportion of Natives who have less than Grade 9 education is twice the national average.

That is a system which does not work.

Beyond that unacceptable human cost, that system nurtures a resentment and suspicion that embitters relations with the larger community. If bitterness prevails, it could be even more difficult to find agreement on questions of land, resource use, and other contentious issues that are central to the development of provinces like British Columbia, Quebec, Alberta.

From one perspective, aboriginal issues raise questions of social and political justice. From another, they reach very close to tensions in our society, which can bring out the worst in all communities. And once confrontation starts, it can prove both durable and contagious. Speaking only for myself, I am surprised that the television coverage of Oka did not inspire more imitation, and that is a risk we want to diminish. We need models of cooperation, not conflict, but they can occur only where there is genuine respect.

The concept of an "inherent" right to self-government is critical, and respect is at its core. First, it accepts the fact that aboriginal people were governing themselves, here, before the rest of us came, and that their right derives from their history, not our discretion. Second, it provides the basis for aboriginal communities to define their future for themselves, and to break a dependency that has proven destructive. But it places responsibility clearly upon those aboriginal communities. Their reputation will be determined by their conduct, by the way they exercise their responsibility.

If that concept is simple, its application is not. I had personally doubted that we could reconcile aboriginal self-government with the need for Canada to speak with one voice in international relations. That particular concern was met by the phrase: "self-government within Canada," which was worked out in the negotiations leading to the Charlottetown Accord.

The referendum debate revealed a broader doubt about precisely how aboriginal governments would work with municipal and provincial authorities. The powers of an aboriginal government would reflect the traditions of that particular community, and since those traditions differ across Canada — from the coastal Haida to the woodland Cree to the Innu — different arrangements would be negotiated in different circumstances. In retrospect, the best way to calm fears about the concept would have been to describe how actual models would work in particular circumstances.

Practicality is not the real obstacle to reforming aboriginal policy. We have the ingenuity to make self-government, and other arrangements, work. The question, as on all constitutional issues, is whether we have the will. That is a question for the aboriginal community, as well as for the rest of us.

During the negotiations, the aboriginal leaders at the table were imaginative, courageous, and sensitive to the problems of others. Because of their history, they came to the table with more suspicions than anyone else, and they were often under acute pressure from their own supporters. Their conduct belied any doubts about whether they could work as equals with other governments. But the constituencies they represent are both complex and unaccustomed to agreement. The question is whether any leadership, however skilled, can draw a durable consensus from the aboriginal community. It would be a tragic irony if the larger community were prepared to change, and the aboriginal community were not able to.

In the larger Canadian community, there is a broad sympathy for the aboriginal people, but that is not the same as respect. The aboriginals are not a Canadian charity. They are a diverse, accomplished, and proud community who, when they were alone on this continent, developed systems and cultures that were more advanced than many in Europe and Asia.

The Iroquois Confederacy is one example. Their system of self-government served as a model for Thomas Jefferson and Benjamin Franklin as they designed the American constitution. The separation of powers, the concept of impeachment, the design of the American federation itself had their parallels in aboriginal governments.

And those accomplishments continue. Even though it was harder to be raised in an Eden Valley than in a High River, aboriginal people are leaders in many Canadian fields, from the rock group Kashtin to the architect Douglas Cardinal, who designed the Museum of Civilization, to the actor Graham Greene, to Nellie Cournoyea, leader of the government of the Northwest Territories, to growing numbers of entrepreneurs, nurses, lawyers, diplomats, teachers, and political leaders. It is natural for them to insist on a Canadian constitution which respects their history and ensures their future.

TEN

QUEBEC

IN THE LATE 1970S, DURING MY EARLY STRUGGLES WITH THE
French language, *Le Devoir* published an editorial "Bloc Note"
which, roughly translated, said: "Mr. Clark is easier to understand in French than Mr. Trudeau. He uses simpler words."

The irony was apt. My spoken French is functional and
unadorned, and my understanding of Quebec is similarly elemental. I am neither a native of the province who learned about
Quebec by growing up there, nor an expert in its culture and
its history. What I know I learned the hard way, as someone
from outside who came to Quebec with an open mind, but a
clear need to understand a community which was very different from my own.

I plunged into the province, studying the French language,
visiting farms and fairs and fishing villages, learning about
people by meeting them. The House of Commons provided an

extraordinary French-language instructor, Claudette Chemla, who would agree that my real instruction was in farmyards in the Eastern Townships, groping for the words to discuss dairy policy with French-speaking farmers, and in question-and-answer sessions after I had ploughed through my formal speech.

Some English Canadians report meeting rudeness in Quebec, or disdain for their halting French. That has to be the exception, not the rule, because, in my early, nearly unilingual forays into Quebec, I was the perfect target for derision. Not only did I speak French like a Martian, but I led a party that, until Robert Stanfield became leader, had been widely perceived as being hostile to Quebec. Yet I was welcomed and encouraged everywhere.

(That is not to say there were no jokes about Joe Clark. Quebec is not that different from the rest of Canada. But even there, the tone was gentle. There is a product called "Clark Beans" that is marketed throughout Quebec and, though I never matched their sales, I was known colloquially as "Joe Bin." That's an improvement on "Joe Who" and, in twenty years on the Quebec stage, as a federalist, an anglophone, and a Progressive Conservative, I was never subject in Quebec to caricatures as harsh as greeted me in English Canada.)

In a sense that is central to my belief that Canada can work, I did not travel in Quebec as a stranger. The more I moved around the province, the more similarities I found with people and attitudes in my own region. The differences are obvious – the language, the landscape, the contrast between a Quebec society hundreds of years old and an Alberta built in this century – and many people, in both communities, never get beyond those differences. Too many never try.

The common ground I found was both personal and political. My party's electoral prospects, such as they were, seemed brighter in rural Quebec than in the cities, so I spent a lot of time in communities that depended, as my Alberta constituency did, on farming and resource development and small business. Those communities were close but not closed. Their events were informal, good-humoured, welcoming, and Maureen and I were accepted into them easily. I remember a Mass on the beach at Paspébiac, on the Gaspé coast. Maureen was to read from the Scripture, and moments before she began, the priest whispered to her: "There's a storm coming. Read it quickly, and I'll wrap this up." Five minutes later, after one of the fastest Masses in Christendom, we were off the beach, and a deluge broke. In fact, our presence had delayed the beginning of that service because it was opened by the local high school choir who, taking account of my prairie origins, offered a bilingual ecumenical participatory hymn. They sang "Oh Susannah," as we might have sung it in Alberta.

Politically, in the late 1970s, the people of Alberta and Quebec both felt themselves a long way from their government in Ottawa. On constitutional questions, the two provinces shared a preference for a federation which left more power with the provinces. Economically, they both believed the real power in the country was somewhere else, probably Ontario, and that their capacity was constrained. The attitude of Albertans and Quebecers had a lot in common. I always had the feeling that High River could fit in either province.

My long immersion in Quebec had some results. A later, kinder editorial in *Le Devoir* called me: "the English-Canadian politician with the best understanding of Quebec." *Le Devoir* today might regard that as the faintest of praise, but I believe I learned things about Quebec that might be useful to other Canadians now.

Many people can afford to ignore parts of Canada they don't know. I couldn't. I was the leader of a national party whose consistent failure to form national governments was rooted in its weakness in Quebec. For my party to succeed, for me to succeed, I had to build some understanding of Quebec.

I think our country is in a similar situation now. For us to succeed as a nation, we have to understand what is driving Quebec.

Obviously, understanding Quebec's motives need not mean supporting Quebec's actions. And, as I argue elsewhere, understanding is a two-way street, and Quebecers also must reach out to the rest of the country. But, as we stand on the doorstep of decisions that could separate Canada, those Canadians who want to keep the country whole have to try to understand those who want to break it up, or those who would go along with breaking it up.

That is an important distinction.

Some Quebecers are convinced separatists. They have thought seriously about independence, and believe they would be better off outside Canada. I can't put a number on that group, but believe it is large and growing. Naturally, it includes some zealots, people who think, and act, in extremes. Every movement has zealots, and some of the most extreme *indépendantistes* are profoundly hostile to Canada. They are influential, because they provide more than their share of the energy which has driven the movement forward. For them, independence is a moral and intellectual imperative, and only the naïve would pretend that they could be reconciled to anything short of separation.

But there is much more to Quebec separatism than those "true believers." There is, tragically, a growing number of calm and rational people who, despite an innate attachment to Canada, have come to the considered view that the larger country either doesn't work at all or doesn't work in their interests. I dispute their assessment, but respect it, because I can understand how, in the last fifteen years, reasonable Quebecers could lose faith in Canada. After all, a small chorus of other Canadians – some business people, some commentators, some economists – have declared the country bankrupt, and their spreadsheets don't even compute factors like the constitutional exclusion of 1982, or the failure of the Meech Lake Accord.

And then, at the core of the separatist movement, is a nationalist sentiment that is as much a part of Quebec as the French language.

English-speaking Canadians don't have much experience with nationalism, as an emotion or as a political movement. From time to time, we have reacted to British or American attempts to impose their policies or their standards. But our form of protest is usually to set up a committee or submit an article. It is almost impossible to visualize thousands of Torontonians filling the streets to defend their culture. Yet that kind of solidarity is commonplace now in Quebec, and there has always been a bond of nationalism in that province. Not every Quebecer has shared it – some find it repugnant. But it is a tangible, continuing characteristic of the Quebec community.

The question of how to deal with Quebec nationalism has divided Canadians who call themselves "federalists." Some genuinely believe that an embrace of Quebec nationalism is a first instalment on separation, and that the better response is to develop pan-Canadian institutions whose appeal is so compelling that they will displace the more parochial nationalism of Quebec.

Part of that assessment makes sense to me. I believe there should be pan-Canadian institutions which encourage Quebecers to feel at home in the larger Canada. But it is naïve to pretend that those institutions can significantly displace the bonds that define a community like Quebec. Those bonds are real and deep and natural. They are part of identity, essential to the self-respect that will allow the Quebec community to be part of the larger Canadian community.

So I see Quebec nationalism as being an asset to Canada, not a threat; a source of confidence, not a slippery slope.

That is a conception of Canada, not just Quebec. Part of the reason the "Canadian identity" is hard to dramatize is that we are a nation of very strong local communities, each with a sure sense of its own identity. That can be divisive, if frustration prevails, whether in Quebec or Calgary or among the Cree. But it is also, everywhere, a source of pride and definition, which can reach outward as easily as it can turn inward. The challenge for Canada is to find ways to encourage citizens who are acutely proud of their own community to take an equal pride in the country.

In Quebec's case, we have not been successful in encouraging the nationalists to reach outwards. On the contrary, the constitutional failures of the last decade have had the opposite effect – they have made it hard for Quebec nationalists to be Canadian federalists. That has given the separatist movement momentum by default. Their ranks are swollen by Quebecers whose natural faith in Canada has become eroded.

The danger is that their numbers could grow again, to include other Quebecers who would regard themselves as both less nationalist and more cautious. Even though they might have nothing against Canada, when jobs are hard to find, and social programs are being cut, and loud English voices are saying "If you want to go, go," and the message from Ottawa is filtered through the Bloc Québécois or the Reform Party, they are likely to see few reasons to stay.

To the degree they think about it, those Quebecers are more

likely to consider themselves unwanted by the larger country. Even if they don't have much personal experience of Canada, outside Quebec, what they have seen or heard recently does not make them feel welcome. Those Quebecers, potential separatists, may not be convinced about independence, but neither are they convinced about Canada.

And they are tired of the debate. Everyone in Canada is tired of the debate, but it has gone on longer in Quebec, without any apparent progress, and it is relatively easy to turn that frustration with the debate into a frustration with Canada.

These issues are never simple, but I believe that large numbers of Quebecers who are strongly tempted by separation would decide to stay in Canada if they believed that other Canadians respected who they are, and wanted them to stay.

Quebec is an unknown country to most Canadians who don't live there. For many years, that was a benign ignorance. As a general rule, in the 1940s and 1950s, Quebec did not intrude much into everyday thinking in Halifax or Toronto or Vancouver, nor was the rest of the country an active presence in much of Quebec. Both the country and the province seemed comfortable in the grip of single-party government – the Liberals in Ottawa, the Union Nationale in Quebec – and there was nothing like the kind of public debate that has become commonplace now. There was a little travel, a little teaching, a little television, a business-like regime in Ottawa, a conservative regime in Quebec, not much contact or contention. But seeds of change were growing, and suddenly they began to blossom.

Some elections just change governments. The Diefenbaker election, in 1957, changed a regime. The outsiders were suddenly in office and, if they stumbled a little, they also brought fundamental changes, and gave Western Canada a prime minister they could identify with. The national party system became competitive for the first time in decades, with the Progressive Conservatives in office, and the Liberal party rebuilding.

A similar, but more profound, transformation was developing in Quebec. Maurice Duplessis died, and his successor as premier, Paul Sauvé, brought a major change in attitude. That was 1959, and I was the editor of the student newspaper, *The Gateway*, at the University of Alberta. The annual conference of the Canadian University Press was in Quebec City that Christmas, and it was my first visit to the province.

That was the week Paul Sauvé died, suddenly, and, even to a transient in *la vielle capitale*, it was clear that more than the man had been lost. Quebec was ready for a major change, and that came when Jean Lesage was elected, and gave effect to "the Quiet Revolution." There were major changes in education, social policy, natural resource development, and the sense that Quebecers could build their own province. The theme was "Maîtres chez nous" ("Masters in our own house"), and it amounted to a transformation of Quebec society, a sudden passage from introspection to confidence, from the past to the future.

Many English Canadians know the phrase "the Quiet Revolution," but not its significance. It marked the end of a passive Quebec, and went beyond words and goals, to bring about actual change, with far-reaching consequences. Those early years of the 1960s saw the Kennedy era in the United States, which, subconsciously, many of us associate with epochal change in social and political attitudes. In fact, and in consequence, the Quiet Revolution in Quebec was a bigger change, and more durable.

I don't think the rest of Canada really knew it was happening, nor yet understands its importance. The story may be apocryphal, but, back in Alberta, I was told that the publisher of one of our leading newspapers had been invited to a conference on the changes in Quebec, and declined, replying: "I know all I need to know about Quebec."

One important characteristic of the Quiet Revolution is that it was driven and led by the government of Quebec. That had little to do with ideology, or the debate, as English Canadians know it, about the role of the private and the public sectors. It speaks instead to how Quebecers see and express themselves, as a minority francophone culture in an anglophone continent.

Quebecers view their province as a whole community, in a way that is unique in Canada. Consequently, they view their provincial government as representing the interests of that whole community, and not simply a political party, or the judgement of an electorate at a particular time.

Putting personalities aside, any government of Quebec is more important to Quebecers than any government of Alberta is to Albertans. Albertans feel independent enough to suspect that governments would try to control their destiny; Quebecers know they are a minority and need to act together to protect their destiny. The government is the expression of the community. That is why constitutional powers assigned to that government are seen as so important in Quebec. And that is why Quebec's absence from federal-provincial and constitutional discussions, after 1982, was such a powerful signal. It was not just the government which stood apart from the process, but the province.

Most Canadians know that Quebec is different. The irony of the controversy over the "distinct society" is that the real debate was not whether it existed, but whether it should be recognized in law. Every Albertan or Nova Scotian or Ontarian whom I ever knew regards Quebec as being different. When your plane lands in Montreal or Quebec City, it doesn't take you long to understand that you are not in Brandon or Buctouche or Toronto – or Paris. And the difference is more than language, although it is rooted there. The culture is different – culture in terms of Anne Hébert and Gilles Vigneault; and culture as the sociologists mean it, embodying the characteristics of the community.

Some of that difference is evident to the naked eye. When I first went to rural Quebec, my High River expectations were jolted by the farmhouses, arrayed side by side, along the river, with each farmer's land stretching back, reflecting the old seigneurial system of France, and distinctly different from the way farms are arranged on my prairies, or in Southern Ontario or the Maritimes.

Other signs are less tangible. I remember the extremely personal reactions of the mourners in the streets, who waved goodbye, as to a friend, when René Lévesque was buried. When Lester Pearson died, and even during that long last train ride home for John Diefenbaker, the crowds were respectful, occasionally distraught, but distant, not intimate. Lévesque is still a part of Quebec society, because it is a close and self-conscious community which needs its heroes as an active presence.

My purpose here is not to try to define the culture, or even describe it, but to register the fact that, when we put our constitutional texts and political preferences aside, most Canadians, in their daily practice, accept the difference of Quebec.

For example, I know a lot of "hands on" Albertans – people who, when they want to know something about another place, go and see for themselves. If they go to Toronto or Victoria or Newfoundland, they develop contacts, but come to their own conclusions.

When they go to Quebec, they look for interlocutors, interpreters, people who can explain what the "hands on"

Albertans realize, instinctively, they can't learn just by digging.

That is the reaction of most Canadians from outside Quebec. I always thought it was one of the reasons why Pierre Trudeau enjoyed such unquestioned authority, outside Quebec, on issues concerning that province. While Quebecers saw him as a controversial actor in the dramas of that province, other Canadians regarded him as the singular authority. In part that was because he was intelligent and articulate, and said things about Quebec which they wanted to believe. But it was also because they had no reference points of their own. They were not at ease in the French language and, if they had visited much in Quebec, had done so as tourists, going where they were pointed, but not acquiring an independent knowledge of their own.

Of course, there are other differences in Canada. Differences are part of our trademark as a country, and some of them are strong and deeply rooted. Unquestionably, there is a Newfoundland culture, and I believe there is a growing Western Canadian consciousness that is much more positive and complex than simple antagonism to the East.

I take nothing away from any of these realities in pointing out that, as a practical matter, Quebec's difference is acknowledged and accepted every day. It is neither new nor threatening. It is a simple fact of life about our country, like the Rocky Mountains, the weather, the effect of the ocean on the Canadians living along the Atlantic coast.

The problem is not the objective reality, but its political recognition. Indeed, that is the problem in a nutshell. Acknowledging a reality is one thing, and writing it into law another. Yet if the reality in question is your own distinct society, and you feel it may be vulnerable, of course you want guarantees that last.

The Quebec difference is more than language, but the

language is key, because it is, literally, the means by which the community tells its story to itself, conveys its values, its images, its roots. In another Canadian context, that is why language is so important to aboriginal people, because it is the essential means to express and extend a culture which might otherwise disappear.

But even this most basic Quebec issue is misunderstood, or seen in other clothes, in the rest of Canada. To many English-speaking Canadians, the "language issue" in Quebec was about the right of English-speaking Quebecers to use English. That was the issue in the headlines, in Calgary and Toronto; that was the principle that seemed threatened by Quebec language laws, and which evoked a powerful fraternal response outside Quebec. Unquestionably, the rights of English-speaking Quebecers should be respected. But the trigger to this controversy was not a threat to the English language in Quebec, but a threat to the French language, and the culture it sustained.

It is not surprising that Quebec would find its language, and therefore its identity, to be vulnerable. Some 280 million people live in North America, north of the Rio Grande. For 7 million of them, largely in Quebec, the everyday language is French; for almost all the rest, the everyday language is English. Those are daunting odds: 270 to 7.

Add two factors. First, the United States, the dominant presence on the continent, is in the business of exporting, everywhere, its values, its styles, its culture, in its language. Naturally, its closest target is next door. That is a challenge, even a threat, to all of Canada, but particularly to the community with the different language, whose kids will be weaned away by the music and images of the overwhelming culture, and by the assumption that, to prosper on this continent, the ticket is the dominant language.

Add to that the immigration of new Canadians, whose first language was neither English nor French, at a time when Quebec's birth rate was going down. New immigrants were choosing English, not French, as their second language, because that was the overwhelmingly dominant language of the continent. Had that trend been ignored, the inevitable result would have been a decline in the use of French as the everyday language of Quebec itself.

One can agree, or disagree, with the means by which Quebec responded to that threat. But no one can deny the threat was real. And it was an elemental threat – going to the heart of the community. To ignore that would be to ignore a basic interest of Quebec. It would be equivalent to an Alberta government surrendering all jurisdiction over oil and natural gas, or an Atlantic government saying "We don't care what happens to the fish stocks." The community of Quebec is a minority in the country, and in the continent. That creates pressures and aspirations that no one can ignore.

ELEVEN

UNDERSTANDING
INDEPENDENCE

THE REAL CHALLENGE, FOR PEOPLE FROM OTHER PARTS OF CANADA, is to stop regarding Quebec separatism largely as a negative force, a reaction against English Canada, a reaction against us. It is hard to be objective about arguments that you take personally.

Unquestionably, some of the deepest roots of Quebec separatism were nourished by anger at the way the English minority treated the French majority in Quebec. There is a French-Canadian folk memory of powerful English-speaking Quebec families who declined to learn French themselves, and who used their considerable influence to look after their own, thus denying opportunities to francophones. Those were "les maudits Anglais."

That reaction is not surprising. Not many Canadians, any-where, would have put up with a powerful minority which consistently demeaned the majority. If that had happened in

Alberta, it would have been resented by its victims there as much as it was in Quebec. But if that is a historic motive of Quebec separatists, it is not particularly powerful today.

The driving force of modern separatism is much more positive. It is, quite simply, a desire to build a new society, and draws more upon pride and confidence than upon resentment or insecurity. In that sense, the motivation is not "anti-English" at all. There is a perverse sense in which English-speaking Canadians would like to be at the centre of the drama in Quebec, but we are not. Modern Quebec separatism is less about breaking away from the English language and culture, and much more about asserting the strengths of the French language and culture which have evolved in North America. It is less a judgement on the success or failure of Canada than a preparation for the success of Quebec.

That is why so many of the leading artists of Quebec embrace the separatist idea, and why it has such powerful appeal to young Quebecers.

Others might dispute the assumptions of separatist leaders, and even accuse them of being naïve. But for us to understand their passion for their cause, we should judge their motivation from their perspective, not just our own.

Most Quebec separatists are serious when they say they have nothing against other Canadians, or the English language, or the culture or ambitions of Toronto, Vancouver, or St. John's. But they have come to the view that their community would be better off on its own.

That is not a surprising aspiration in North America. The Thirteen Colonies founded a nation on such a dream and, for literally millions of families, that was the personal purpose in coming to North America.

So the challenge for those of us who want to keep Canada whole is to make two distinct, but legitimate, cases to Quebec.

The first case, to be made as proponents of Canada, is that Quebecers would find more room to grow, as individuals and as a community, in the large country Canada has become than it would in a fledgling venture of its own.

The second case, to be made as sceptics about separatism, is that breaking the Canadian federation would have costs and consequences for us all. In other chapters, I raise some considerations about those costs – to Quebec, to Alberta, to individuals; indeed, to the international community.

But my real interest is in the first case.

I see three realities linked closely together.

The first is that Quebec cannot accept the status quo in Canada, and that, indeed, the changes proposed in both the Meech Lake and the Charlottetown accord will not now be enough to give Quebec reasonable confidence that it can flourish in Canada.

Second, the so-called Quebec question is only one of several issues that require Canadians to consider basic changes in our approach to public policy. There are, of course, the other urgent "constitutional" issues of the Canada Round. But, beyond that, other areas of contemporary Canadian policy are based upon premises that no longer apply, and new issues are ignored in an atmosphere fixated on fiscal restraint. In other words, more needs changing than the constitution.

Third, there is a surprising will to change in Canada. Its focus is scattered now: some insist our future depends upon severe fiscal restraint; others urge that education is the priority, or our competitiveness in the world, or constitutional reform. But no one is wedded to the status quo. And no one serious pretends the issues are easy.

This country has come a long way without focusing specifically on the goals it should pursue in common. Particular governments have had activist agendas in several fields, but there has never been a time when the whole Canadian community set out to discuss and pursue specific national goals. In one sense, that is against our pragmatic character and history.

But, here we are, in 1994, with a debt that threatens our future and inhibits initiative, a province actively considering separation, a social policy which, while widely admired, simultaneously nourishes dependency and can't respond adequately to new issues, and a political atmosphere dominated by frustration and a good measure of snake oil.

Is there a way for us to channel the dynamic energies which are pulling us steadily apart and direct them towards a broad Canadian renewal?

TWELVE

"SPECIAL STATUS"

THE DEBATE ABOUT THE "DISTINCT SOCIETY" BECAME CONTROVERsial because many Canadians thought it would confer rights on Quebec that other provinces did not enjoy. That raised a complicated issue because, in fact, Canada's system of federalism has always recognized differences among provinces. In fact, there would never have been Confederation without a willingness to recognize the differences of the founding provinces, including in the language of the constitution.

In Canada, there is a fundamental distinction between uniformity and equality. Equality is a basic and enduring Canadian value. More than simply being reflected in our constitution and our law, it is part of our sense of ourselves. Canadians do not like the idea of second-class citizens, nor, when we think about it, of second-class provinces. We believe that part of the definition of our special country is our respect for the values of fairness, justice, and equality. Indeed, our challenge is to make those principles effective for all the people of Canada, so that individuals are not denied them by the barriers of poverty, or sexual or racial or other discrimination. Some of the most important debates in Canada are about the means to define, and the means to achieve, real equality.

But one thing is clear. In Canada, equality has never meant uniformity – and, indeed, uniformity often means inequality, because it does not take account of real differences. That rule applies to provinces, as well as to people. Our system of equalization does not treat provinces as though they are uniform. On the contrary: it was created because some provinces were too poor to provide an adequate level of services for the Canadians who lived there. My own province was one of the early beneficiaries of equalization, because that principle was established before the discovery of oil at Leduc. Alberta is a wealthy province now, with a rich resource base, but we were one of the "have-not" provinces that the equalization principle was designed to help. That principle recognizes that the naturally richer provinces have an obligation to help others, precisely to achieve a greater equality of opportunity for all the people and provinces of Canada.

The logic and genius of Canadian federalism are that provinces are to be equal in status, but able to meet the unique needs of their people. And that principle is not new. It is as old as the country.

Four existing colonies formed Confederation – Upper Canada, which became Ontario; Lower Canada, which became Quebec; Nova Scotia; and New Brunswick. If those four communities had been uniform – with the same resources, the same language, the same religion, the same size – there would have been no need for a federal system. They could have established a unitary state, with one government. But the colonies were not uniform; they had differences. They needed a system which established equal rights but recognized different needs. That is what a federal system means. The Canadian confederation was invented to allow different communities to work together.

Two of those founding colonies wanted the right to denominational schools to be spelled out – so that right was established for Ontario and Quebec, and not for New Brunswick and Nova Scotia. Representation in Parliament was not the same, because the founding communities were of different sizes. The Civil Code was established for Quebec, but was not imposed upon the other provinces. So, from the very beginning of the country, we have recognized differences among provinces.

That practice continued as Confederation grew. The terms of union for the six provinces which joined Confederation after 1867 were different. Prince Edward Island required an undertaking about ferry services. British Columbia was promised a railway. Manitoba undertook to provide a bilingual legislative and court system. Alberta and Saskatchewan were, for a long time, denied the full right to develop their natural resources. Newfoundland secured assurances regarding its unique education system.

Even today, the powers exercised by the governments of the Yukon and the Northwest Territories are less than those of full provinces, but more than they used to be. So there have always been differences, and they have always affected other provinces, as well as Quebec.

If you choose to use the term, you could say there is "special status" for Newfoundland because there are special constitutional guarantees respecting its schools. Similarly, there is "special status" for denominational schools in Ontario, as in Quebec; "special status" for P.E.I. respecting the ferry guarantees; "special status" for Manitoba regarding language in the legislature and courts.

But that is not the way the term has been used in Canada recently. The words "special status" became a code, not to describe the enduring genius of Canadian Confederation, but to imply privilege for Quebec. That became a major issue when many Canadians were uncomfortable with what they saw of the Meech Lake Accord and searched for arguments that would express or justify their concern. In the ensuing political controversy, what mattered was not the history, which most people didn't know or much care about, but the perception that a special status was being created, and conferred freshly upon Quebec.

That became a stumbling block to one of the creative proposals which might have been the basis of an agreement. In January 1992, the first of the series of "policy conferences" on the constitution was held in Halifax. It was the trial run of an experiment that drew together elected officials, so-called experts, representatives of various interest groups, and Canadian citizens who had written in to apply to participate. A consensus emerged in favour of what was called "asymmetrical federalism." The idea behind that awkward phrase was the reapplication, in 1992, of the long-established Canadian practice of recognizing that different provinces have different needs. In this case, it would have recognized the unusual importance of cultural questions to Quebec, and given Quebec certain powers respecting culture that would not be available to other provinces. The alternative was to grant greater powers to all the provinces, and many participants in the Halifax conference thought that would weaken Canada's central government unacceptably.

Logically, no Canadian should object to "asymmetrical federalism." In principle, it is the system we have always had.

So, after the Halifax conference, I began immediately to ask leaders of provincial governments whether they could accept this established principle, applied narrowly and specifically to cultural questions and Quebec. In fact, I broadened the inquiry to include leaders of opposition parties, in most jurisdictions, because this had become essentially a political problem, and I was looking for help in finding ways to make it work. The principle was sound. It had worked before. It was part of the Canadian tradition. Could we build acceptance for that approach to culture now? The answer, consistently, was no, often not because of a lack of will, but because, in 1992, that established principle was seen to mean "special status for Quebec," and I couldn't find any government, outside Quebec, which thought it could sell that concept to its voters.

In future discussions, that political atmosphere may change, particularly if we succeed in making the distinction between equality and uniformity. The Halifax idea of "asymmetrical federalism" is perfectly sound. But, in a negotiation, good ideas are useful only if you can make them work; that is what is meant by politics being the "art of the possible." We need to spend more time helping Canadians know more about how our country developed, and take the fear away from phrases like "special status."

The related phrase which set off alarm bells was "the distinct society." That innocent set of words suddenly became a symbol. To Quebecers, that phrase expressed a long-delayed recognition, in the constitution, of a reality that had existed for centuries. To many outside Quebec, it was alarming proof of privilege and special status. The aboriginal people, not unreasonably, believed that innocent set of words applied to them as much as to anyone, and one of my early tug-of-wars with Ovide Mercredi, the National Chief of the Assembly of First Nations, occurred when I asked him to accept the political reality that, in this negotiation, Quebec had first call on that phrase.

(I have a very high regard for Ovide Mercredi and always tried to demonstrate my respect for his office and for him. But he had gone to Quebec to announce that aboriginals were the real "distinct society," and, in a meeting with AFN leaders, I lost my temper and said: "Ovide, trying to follow your argument is like following a kid on a tricycle on ice." Everyone in the room was briefly embarrassed and, of course, the story leaked to the press. Months later, when we were on the edge of agreeing to the Charlottetown Accord, Ovide presented me with a tiny toy tricycle, reminding me that we had come across a lot of ice together.)

In a strict sense, every province in Canada is distinct, not just because each is different from the others, but because those differences form a culture, a character, a community. There is a British Columbia identity, a Nova Scotia identity, a Saskatchewan identity. But, in that sense, Quebec is doubly distinct, and has been, literally, for more than two centuries.

The "distinct society" was recognized in law, in 1774, by the Parliament of Great Britain, when it passed the Quebec Act. That established the legal, or "official," status of the French language in what was to become Canada, and the distinct system of land ownership, and a distinct legal system, based on the Code Napoléon. That was 220 years ago, nearly a century before Confederation.

When the Parliament at Westminster passed the Constitutional Act, to create Upper Canada and Lower Canada, in 1791, those "distinct society" provisions were retained. That tradition was continued by Canada's Fathers of Confederation, in 1867. The British North America Act recognized the Civil Code in Quebec, the only province in which that form of law was to be used. It granted the use of French and English in the courts and legislatures of Quebec, as it did not in the other founding provinces. It established distinct provisions respecting the appointment of senators and judges in Quebec, different from the provisions in other provinces.

In fact, the Fathers of Confederation had a stronger reason than tradition for ensuring that the BNA Act reflected the "distinct society" of Quebec. It was a more pragmatic reason: there had been an earlier attempt to deny the "distinct society" and it had failed.

Lord Durham's famous report had described Canada as "two nations warring in the bosom of a single state" and recommended that French Canadians be assimilated. Westminster was persuaded by his argument and, in the Act of Union of 1840, created a single province out of Upper and Lower Canada. That experiment did not work.

Being practical people, the Fathers of Confederation changed the failed system to reflect reality. They understood that, if Canada was to continue, it had to adopt a political structure which would accommodate the distinct nature of Quebec in a growing country. Confederation was the result. A federal system was adopted. Provinces were created, with their own separate powers and their own institutions. In effect, the very origins of the country lay in the failure of efforts to ignore or extinguish the distinctness of Quebec.

That history matters to more than Quebec, because it produced a Canada in which all provinces, Alberta as well as Quebec, had more power than they might have had. Most of the Fathers of Confederation – including Sir John A. Macdonald – preferred a more centralized country. Had they been building a theoretical model, they would have put more power in Ottawa, and left less to the provinces. But they were building a country, not a theory, and they had to take account of the reality of Canadian diversity, whose most compelling example and exponent, at the time, was the "distinct society" of French Canada.

In my home region, in Western Canada, there is sometimes a temptation to treat Western history as separate from the history of the country, and Western interests as being hostile to those of Quebec. Certainly some interests in the West are different from Quebec's. Just as certainly, there are aspects of the Western Canadian experience that did not occur in other parts of Canada, and are not adequately reflected or respected in most versions of the Canadian story. That is part of the reason why Western Canadians "feel misunderstood."

But it is one thing to argue that there is a distinct Western Canadian experience and identity, and quite another to seek to disconnect the West from the country. To do so disconnects the West from itself, from a critical part of its own history. The Confederation agreement did not merely create the country which Western provinces joined, it created the kind of country that gave room to Western provinces to express their difference.

There is a direct relation between the need to embrace the "distinct society" of French Canada and the view that it is appropriate for Western provinces to control their own natural resources, education, and other fields which define identity. Canada's provinces, as jurisdictions, are more powerful than the individual American states of the federation next door. One reason for the difference is that there was no Quebec in the thirteen colonies who formed the first American union, no community arguing for the room to be different. In that sense, it was Quebec who defended the interests of Western Canada in the Confederation discussions, and it was the "distinct society" of French Canada that made possible the kind of Confederation that gives Western provinces more power in Canada than Western states enjoy in the United States.

Why does this argument matter? It matters because the discussion about Canada has become distorted by an exaggeration of our differences, and a slighting of the interests and attitudes we share. That has occurred everywhere in Canada, but is most marked in Quebec and the West.

Most Quebecers, in my experience, know less about Western Canada than they do about Ontario or the Atlantic provinces, where there are closer connections of family or language or geography. It is easier to go to Moncton than to Manitoba. Quebecers like the idea of the Rocky Mountains or the Pacific coast, but not many actually come to see them. The West was not part of the original Confederation and, both literally and symbolically, seems the most distant from Quebec.

Moreover, in the last twenty years, the West has changed almost as much as Quebec, not least in its sense of its own strength and potential. That should have created a common bond between the two regions. Despite their distance from each other, and their cultural difference, Quebec and Western Canada shared a common interest in redefining the country Canada was becoming. They both strained against Toronto's dominance of Canadian economic decisions. They shared a desire to have national institutions reflect more of their identity and, on most of the constitutional issues of the last two decades, the two provinces who were most often allies were Alberta and Quebec.

The profound changes in their own province meant that most Quebecers were too absorbed by their own society to pay much attention to Western Canada, or, what was worse, to consider it as being significantly different from Ontario. So there was a double problem of perception: the images of the West in Quebec were never particularly strong or accurate, and those images stayed static as the West changed. The result was not hostility towards the West, but an indifference to changes which Western Canadians themselves thought were significant.

The Western Canadian attitude to Quebec is more complex, but it is certainly not indifference. On the contrary: indifference to Quebec is a luxury most Western Canadians feel they cannot indulge — for two opposing reasons. In one camp are people who fear the departure of Quebec would imperil their country, and want Quebec to stay. In another camp are people who believe it is the preoccupation with Quebec which imperils the country. In fact, many Western Canadians belong to both camps, but there is a steady increase in irritation with Quebec, and that trend was given momentum by the notion that the "distinct society" was another form of "special status" for Quebec.

THIRTEEN

WHAT DOES
CANADA WANT?

I MAKE A BASIC ASSUMPTION ABOUT OUR CHALLENGE TODAY, AND
it should be stated clearly – that is, that the real question is not
about the future of Quebec, but about the nature of Canada.
And while Quebecers, as Canadians, should have a strong voice
in the response, that is a question for all Canadians, a question
to which, ideally, a clear answer should begin to be evident before
any referendum is held in Quebec.

If there is another Quebec referendum, that will be a matter
for Quebecers. Canadians from elsewhere will express our
views, as I and others did in 1980, as we have a right to, in a
free society, when our interests are at stake. But, in such a case,
the debate would be one thing, the decision another.

The decision about staying in Canada is for Quebec to make.
The terms of separation, if it came to that, would be subject
to a negotiation that would almost certainly be ugly and

incapacitating. But it is idle to dispute the right of Quebecers to decide to leave Canada. As a practical matter, if a province wants to leave, there is nothing the rest of Canada can do to hold it where it doesn't want to be.

On the other hand, it is both appropriate, and necessary, for other Canadians to make Canada a place where Quebec would choose to be, choose to stay. That should not be done in terms of enticements to Quebec, but rather on the basis of the objective merits of Canada.

Part of the case *for* Canada is a bread-and-butter issue – the economic advantages, to Quebec and to Canada, of staying one large country, and the costs, to Quebec and to Canada, of separation. But, at heart, this is not an issue of economics, nor is it one of "bargaining." It is an issue of the kind of community we are, and want to be, and can become. It is about the nature of the country of which we are asking Quebec to be part.

In June 1990, on the night the Meech Lake Accord failed, then premier Robert Bourassa said, in the National Assembly of Quebec: "Until 1985, the question was: what does Quebec want? Since then, the question is: what does Canada want?"

That is still the question, and it would be worth asking even if there were no referendum, no threat of separation. What does Canada want? In what kind of community are we asking Quebecers to take part? What does that Canada offer Western Canadians? What does it offer "new" Canadians?

At least since the Quiet Revolution, Quebec has had a clear sense of who it is as a community, and what it wants to do. The Quiet Revolution was a watershed, distinguishing a passive Quebec from the self-confident society that took its schools back from the Roman Catholic Church, established Hydro-Québec, opened offices around the world, spawned the companies that became known as "Quebec Inc.," and became an assertive presence in the country.

In the larger Canadian community, there has been no such watershed, and there is no similar sense of strong identity or compelling purpose. Obviously that cannot be created artificially, and it is harder to evoke in a massive country than it is in a province set apart by its language and culture. But if Canada wants to hold Quebec, wants to hold the West, wants "new" Canadians to prize the country they are joining, the sense of Canada must be as positive and compelling to Canadians as the sense of Quebec is today to Quebecers.

I think that can happen – because there is a real and tangible Canadian community. I know that because, for the last thirty years, I have poked into the corners of this distinctive country, seen its people in triumph, and in stress, and in repose. There is a society here – dare I say a "distinct" society – with characteristics that are common across our vast geography, and different from those of any other community in the world.

Think of some simple things.

Saskatchewan believes its co-op movement helps define Saskatchewan. Quebec believes "les caisses populaires" help define Quebec. Nova Scotians boast about the Coady Institute. The credit unions are deep in the history of Ontario. Those are all the same thing. Is their importance merely local? Or are they Canadian, reflecting characteristics that develop naturally across this community?

How is it that we have national programs of medical care, and hospital insurance, and unemployment insurance? Did some tricky politician impose something that was against our nature? On the contrary.

Think of hockey. The names change across the generations.

But "Conacher" and "The Rocket" and "Howe" and "Gretzky" were, each in his time, names that inspired the same awe, in French or English or Ukrainian, on corner rinks and in bars across the country. Our hockey heroes might have been born in Russia or played in Detroit, but they are ours. The game is ours, even when we lose.

Think of the North. Most of us have never been there, except in our imagination, but the images of space and ice and solitude are as native to us as the palm tree is to the Polynesian.

Think of the police. They have a tough job, and sometimes make mistakes. But Canadians, generally, trust the police, respect their function. The phrase is not as ringing as "Liberté, égalité, fraternité" but there is something sensible and right about a system dedicated to "peace, order and good government."

This is a real country, and it is about more than just politics and laws and economics. Canada is a place people love, and belong to. It is our home.

Our problem, as Canadians, is that we don't talk and think enough about that country. That is also one of our attractions, both in the world, where we are so respected, and at home, where people are free to live their lives undemonstratively.

But we have been so silent that we have almost come to believe that there is no country here. That belief could become self-fulfilling, unless we put our country back in view.

That is not a complicated thing to do. For example, we need, deliberately, to tell one another Canadian stories. I don't just mean history, although I am astounded at how little Canadians know about how the country came to be. I mean everyday things. Where do the kids in the rocky outport towns of Newfoundland play baseball? Would you be able to order a meal in small-town Quebec if you didn't speak French? What exactly are the Northern Lights? Where did Wayne and Shuster go to school?

Those topics are not selected at random. I was told all those things, and thousands more, in casual conversations with Canadians over the last thirty years. The country is full of stories we don't bother telling one another and which, if known, would change our understanding of our neighbours.

One of the reasons it is such a privilege to be a member of Parliament is that you push aside that Canadian reserve, and learn that there is real meaning to the qualities people associate with Canada. Take, for example, how profoundly people in many countries fear their government, and how differently authority is exercised here.

When I first ran for Parliament, my constituency included a community that was "East Coleman" on the map, but "Bushtown" to everyone else. It is in the Crows Nest Pass, and coal miners and their families lived there, many of them originally from Eastern Europe.

I went door to door, looking for votes, and one Saturday morning was surprised to be told, four or five times, at different houses: "You seem like a nice young man, but I can't vote for you."

I finally asked: "Why not?" and was told that, during the Depression, there were violent miners' strikes, and the family names of people who demonstrated were noted, and made their way into files in Ottawa. Years later, when people with those names applied for Canadian citizenship, they were told there was a mark on their file.

In their countries of origin, a mark on the file could be fatal, so they withdrew their applications. One woman said: "I would like to die a citizen of the country where I have lived my life." When I told Canadian citizenship officials that story, they arranged a special court in Bushtown, where thirteen long-time Canadians became citizens.

Yet, our stories alone are not enough. We need to talk more to one another about our goals, what we want to become. Our ubiquitous southern neighbour, and some other countries, do that as a matter of course. We do it rarely, as a whole country, so assume either that we have no goals or that we have none in common. We focus passionately on our differences, and not enough on our shared history and achievements.

Ironically, our differences are minor compared with the hatred and suspicion that rend other societies. In a world of Pol Pot and apartheid, Bosnia and Rwanda, the Middle East and the Mujahidin, the Golden Temple and East Los Angeles, Canada's conflicts don't even register on the Richter scale. But they are steadily corroding the country.

I have had a unique opportunity to assess this corrosion, and to see it in the context of other societies. For nearly seven years, as Canada's foreign minister, I was exposed directly both to the conflicts in other societies, and to their unqualified envy of Canada.

On Canada's behalf, I visited refugee camps in Indo-China, the Middle East, Central America, and Pakistan. Maureen met the Mothers of the Disappeared in Argentina, children wasted by disease in West Africa, Cambodian infants dismembered by stray land mines. I chaired a Commonwealth committee seeking agreement in southern Africa, worked with Palestinians wanting the security of a homeland, and sent Canadian advisers to help other societies write constitutions, or protect human rights, or learn to keep peace. And everywhere, the Canadian contribution was not just the money that was brought, or the advice, or the comfort, but also the example, the Canadian example, the proof that, in this world, different people can live in harmony.

And then I was called home, to where the harmony had stopped. My formal job was to seek agreement on constitutional changes and, in the process, I was thrown back into intimate contact with my country.

People were extremely generous, with their time – and with their advice. Indian elders, who had voted to exclude "white men" from their pipe ceremonies, made an exception in my case, to help me understand their traditions. Premiers, who were in bitter conflict with my government, opened their homes and, I think, their hearts to me. Quebec separatists, who profoundly opposed my mission, treated me with unfailing courtesy. And, in open meetings across the land, thousands of Canadians talked with me about our country.

Those conversations revealed their share of sharp differences, bitter anger, surprising ignorance, and, sometimes, resentment and fear. But I found very little that should cause a country to come apart, and nothing that would justify losing this remarkable community.

What I found instead is a widespread sense that Canada is valuable, and a widespread love of country – but no consensus on what that country is, or how it might be saved.

FOURTEEN

WHAT DID THE
FAILURES TEACH US?

DEFEAT IS PART OF PUBLIC LIFE, AND I HAVE KNOWN MY SHARE OF it. The public ritual of politics requires you to get up smiling, but it's hard to lose – hard both personally, and because you can't help thinking about the attitudes and opportunities you brought down with you.

Elections make a vast difference – whether in the future of a country or in the nature of a party – and that was certainly true of those I lost, in the general election of 1980 and, then, in my party, in 1983.

But, at the time, neither of those distressed me as much as the referendum deafeat of the Charlottetown Accord.

I had simply assumed that my country would survive with another prime minister, and my party with another leader. I had no such confidence that Canada would survive, after the rejection of the Charlottetown Accord. The public debate had revealed such depths of misunderstanding and hostility that I could not see how we could bring Canadians together in time to meet the inevitability of some new challenge in Quebec.

No one wants a long review of recent constitutional history. But four points are worth making about the Charlottetown Accord and its rejection in the 1992 referendum.

First, technically, what failed in the Charlottetown process was the referendum, not the negotiation. The negotiation succeeded — and it was an extraordinary success, achieving unanimity among seventeen very different parties, on an exceptionally broad agenda.

But more notable than its scope and unanimity is the fact that the agreement was real — it happened because reasonable people took the time to listen to one another and find common ground. There was no magic, no manipulation.

There is a mystique about negotiations. They are seen as a pressure-cooker, where talk is fast, and arms are twisted, and deals are cut that won't stand scrutiny. That is only partly true. There is pressure, because, by definition, new agreements mean changing old positions, and that almost always requires some persuasion. Most agreements, of any kind, are reached under pressure, and often those agreements prove both sound and durable. Personally, I am convinced that the Meech Lake Accord would have met that test, if it had gone on to be approved by the legislatures of Newfoundland and Manitoba. My view has always been that the fatal objections to that accord had more to do with style than with substance. Television has transformed public life, giving every citizen an aisle seat, and, in that long June week in 1991, when the leaders of Canada disappeared each day into the dark maw of the conference centre in Ottawa, Canadians did not like what they saw. A sense developed that, while that atmosphere may be acceptable for the negotiation of ordinary matters, it was not appropriate for a constitution. That image corroded public support for both that agreement and the process of constitutional discussion. Any new negotiation would have to take a different approach.

So our meetings were straightforward and unscripted. We had a purpose, and an agenda, but no precooked results. Those discussions started uneasily. The several memories of Meech Lake cast long shadows, but we were able to build both trust and agreement, because all parties came to take the others seriously. I am convinced we could achieve a similar result in the country at large if we could find a way for Canadians to speak as directly to one another as their leaders did in that process.

The second point is that, whether they agreed or disagreed with the particular solutions proposed in the Charlottetown Accord, most Canadians accepted that the basic problems it addressed are real, and need to be resolved. Some would add other issues. But, if there was disagreement about the remedies proposed at Charlottetown, there is no real disagreement about the agenda, and a country with a broad consensus on agenda is a country with a future. Canada's citizens are not divided on fundamental principles, as the citizens of some countries are.

Third, hundreds of thousands of Canadians became actively involved in the debate. Obviously some of those who opposed the accord, particularly in Quebec, have lost faith in Canada. But many Canadians who couldn't bring themselves to support the accord are profoundly patriotic Canadians, and certainly would work to keep the country together.

The Charlottetown Accord was the tangible product, which was judged, and found wanting, in the referendum. But a constitution is one thing, and the country is something more. The debate generated a dynamic of its own and, perhaps uniquely in our national history, caused large numbers of Canadians to become personally involved in considering a common set of questions about Canada.

There have, of course, been Canadian debates before – on the "National Policy," conscription, the pipeline, the flag, the Free Trade Agreement. In a sense, they were all debates about the nature of Canada, and some of them evoked broad participation.

But they each had a more specific focus, and none of them generated the extent of personal grass-roots engagement that led three-quarters of the population of Canada to go out and vote on a cold October day.

The Charlottetown discussions really were a Canada Round, not simply in their attempt to involve several parties, but in the response they evoked among Canadians.

Finally, the referendum vote was influenced by several factors which had little to do with either the contents of the accord or a judgement on the future of the country. There was a general cynicism about politics, which reached well beyond Canada. Just days after our referendum vote, more than 19 million Americans voted, in their own presidential election, for a Ross Perot candidacy that was, essentially, a run against the system. Incumbent governments from Paris to Tokyo to Moscow were in trouble with their populations, to the point where one could argue that what was unpopular was government itself. But, whatever the weight of larger trends, there was also a particular antagonism to the Progressive Conservative government of Canada. I suspect that had as much to do with issues like the Goods and Services Tax as it did with constitutional questions themselves, but it was a tangible factor in my public meetings, particularly in Western Canada, and as the campaign drew to a

close. One evening in Courtenay, on Vancouver Island, an articulate woman said: "I don't understand why we are doing it this
way. We elect politicians to make decisions, and you have considered this carefully and made a decision. I trust my politicians."
The crowd was stunned into silence by that last sentence. In
other times, a unanimous agreement, one that included aboriginal leaders, would have long coat-tails, but in 1992, that very
unanimity was suspect.

Undoubtedly, the organized opposition of the "No" campaign made a difference. In particular, outside Quebec, Pierre
Trudeau's opposition to Charlottetown swung a lot of votes.

Campaigns have lives of their own and, once a slide starts,
it is hard to stop. The Charlottetown Accord was complex, and
included concepts that were new and sometimes startling. Why
should Quebec surrender its advantage in the Senate? Why
should Ontario? What exactly does "aboriginal self-government" mean? Each detail was a point for the critics to poke, and,
as general doubts rose about the whole proposal, specific reservations became more compelling. We had needed a large package
to get any agreement at all, but once the campaign began to slide,
the size of the package hastened its fall.

In my view, there was one other decisive factor, and that
was the tone of the "Yes" campaign. Unfortunately, part of the
legacy of the Meech Lake process is that a suspicion of manipulation hangs over constitutional questions. During the Charlottetown negotiation itself, and in the period before the formal
negotiation began, we worked deliberately to overcome that suspicion. By and large, that succeeded, and the public seemed prepared to give their governments the benefit of the doubt. The
referendum was conducted under very difficult time constraints,
and a decision was taken to rely on the traditional means of

persuasion. With the added benefit of hindsight, the "Yes" campaign in the referendum would have been more successful had it focused more on the contents of the accord and on the way agreement was achieved.

I can't assign a vote weight to those factors — cynicism, complexity, specific opponents, and the tone of the campaign. But my guess is that, together, those factors made the difference between "Yes" and "No." None of them is a constant in constitutional discussions. Certainly, no one should treat a referendum, conducted in the unusual circumstances of late 1992, as a final judgement on the country.

FIFTEEN

THE ANGER IN CANADA

THERE IS NO RULE THAT SAYS EVERY COUNTRY SHOULD SUCCEED, and none that requires failed countries to stay together. Divorce is acceptable in international relations. So no one argues that Canada should stay together just because it is here.

But longevity and success should count for something. The country has existed for 127 years. It has one of the highest standards of living in the world, and one of the most advanced and comprehensive social systems. It is peaceful, orderly, and with a high degree of personal freedom. It is widely admired. If those qualities were up for auction, most of the world would bid. They are not the sorts of advantages one throws away casually.

So, it is reasonable to argue that the burden of proof does not rest with people who want to continue the Canadian success, but rather with those who would break up the country, or acquiesce in its break-up.

Of course, we should be sure that the assets and advantages we claim for Canada are real. By the same token, we should be sure that the liabilities that are claimed are also real, and that they justify discarding a country that has worked longer and better than most.

Sir Wilfrid Laurier used to talk about "sunny ways." He was not referring to the weather, but to the attitude we take to our problems. By that standard, we have been living through stormy times, in Canada, and in most developed societies, for the last several years. Factories have closed, jobs have been lost, settled values have been challenged, and, perhaps most important in countries like Canada, the edge has been taken off our optimism. For most of Canada's history, parents assumed that life would be better for their children than it had been for them; suddenly that proposition seems in doubt, and so are other assumptions we took for granted. Most Canadians are uneasy; many are angry.

Those are not the best circumstances in which to provoke discussion of a constitution. Ideally, that kind of challenge should be undertaken when people are in a generous frame of mind, looking forward, optimistic. Those are not the adjectives to describe the attitudes I found among Canadians during my long series of public and private meetings in 1991 and 1992.

There are some advantages to anger. People speak their feelings, unrestricted by a sense of politeness or propriety. So, as I listened to Canadians across our country, I met a lot of frankness and frustration, particularly in Western Canada, where, during the referendum campaign, I spent much of my time.

What was interesting was the focus of that anger. Naturally, a lot of it was specific, aimed at the Goods and Services Tax and the Mulroney government. But, more generically, it was a complaint about government – it cost too much, was too complicated, was beholden to narrow interests, didn't solve the problems it promised to solve. If I had been travelling across the United States, or the United Kingdom, or anywhere else in Western Europe, in 1991 or 1992, I would have heard the same generic complaints. They reflect a frustration with contemporary democratic governance, not with Canadian federalism.

Yet, in Canada, because everything has a constitutional edge, and we were involved in a constitutional debate, those complaints were interpreted as pointing to faults in the country itself.

It is hard to make rational decisions in a climate like that. Some of Canada's basic problems are constitutional – familiar issues like the recognition of Quebec as a distinct society, institutional reform, aboriginal self-government, and, almost inevitably now, which government exercises which powers. That will mean major constitutional changes, some sooner and some later, and each change will generate real debate. My judgement, as a veteran of those wars, is that we can find acceptable solutions to the constitutional questions, on their merits. The challenge will be to cut through the thicket of emotion that has been cultivated around the constitution, particularly when there is a growing sense of pessimism about Canada's prospects.

Unquestionably, that pessimism was deepened by the results of the 1993 federal general election, which means that Canada's divisions are reflected sharply, indeed exaggerated, in the House of Commons. But that too should be seen in perspective. Western Canada periodically elects regional parties – the Progressives, the CCF, Social Credit, now Reform. The result in Quebec in 1993 was much more unusual because, for years, parties that won majorities in Canada also won majorities in Quebec.

But the election of two regional parties should not obscure the fact that Jean Chrétien's government enjoys a solid majority in Parliament, and strong representation from every province and territory. It is a genuinely national government, with a pan-Canadian mandate.

Moreover, while their number of seats in Parliament was reduced dramatically, the Progressive Conservative and New Democratic parties, won, respectively, 16 and 6 per cent of the popular vote in that election. They are both much closer to the federalism of the Liberal party than they are to the extreme views of Canada expressed by the two regional parties.

There has been an ironic symmetry to some of the resentments that gnaw at Canada.

A special place in the catalogue of Western Canadian frustration is reserved for Quebec, because many Western Canadians believe the reason their government works badly is that its priorities have been captured by Quebec. Coupled with the West's historic suspicion of the central government, those factors encourage the view in Western Canada that, without Quebec's hidden hand and heavy demands, Canadian government would be cheaper, more straightforward, less corrupt.

Not surprisingly, the separatists in Quebec use a similar argument to advance separation – they blame Canada for the debt, and taxes, and frustrations which unsettle so many Quebecers.

So, in the West, the culprit is Quebec; in Quebec, the culprit is Canada. Such is the power of the politics of frustration.

It is fair enough, in our democracies, that political frustration should bring down governments. But the result in Canada could be to bring down a country, often for reasons that have little to do with the worth or nature of Canada.

Looking back on the failure of the Charlottetown Accord in the 1992 referendum, one might argue that we should have left the constitution alone, and not run the risk of having Canadians take out their anger on the country. That is a beguiling theory but, in my view, was never a realistic option.

The issues could not be ducked. A referendum was set in Quebec, for June or October of 1992, and could not be avoided or delayed. The question in that referendum would be a judgement either on a new constitutional proposal or on a federation that had rejected the Meech Lake Accord. On the first question, Canada had a chance of winning; on the second, it had none. The do-nothing option was guaranteed to bring a crisis. So we had to try a new agreement, despite the risks.

No one was more conscious of those risks than I was. I come from the part of Canada where the anger with Quebec, and the frustration with government, were most palpable. I also knew that many of the most convinced federalists in Quebec regarded the failure of the Meech Lake Accord as a personal rejection, which corroded their confidence in federalism.

And while others might have the luxury of contemplating our dilemma from some sideline, I had been named the "minister responsible" for finding a solution.

In another chapter, I argue that, while the accord failed, the actual negotiation succeeded. I know that sounds like saying: "The operation was a success, but the patient died." Yet nothing has died except a proposal. The future of the country is still to be decided, although that question is looming.

The issue now is whether the memories of failure, out of Charlottetown, will outweigh the lessons of success. Because the truth is that, even in a period of unusual anger and frustration, Canadian leaders came to an agreement, unanimously, on a very complex package, and many Canadian citizens, outside Quebec, asked themselves the question "What does Canada mean to me?" and became more committed to their country.

Naturally enough, those successes have been overshadowed by the stark reality that the venture failed. Nonetheless, the successes were real. They happened in a hostile climate, and they challenge the notion that the country is fated to fail. They argue, in fact, that there is a natural community in Canada, if we bother to bring it out.

SIXTEEN

RESPECT

BY THE STANDARDS OF MOST OF THE COUNTRIES IN THE WORLD, Canada's basic disagreements are pretty modest.

Martial Asselin, now the lieutenant-governor of Quebec, was the minister responsible for international development in "le gouvernement éphémère" of 1979-80. He was travelling in Africa the night that government was defeated, and was awakened by his very anxious host, who said: "There has been a *coup d'état* in your country. Such an odd country. Two *coups d'état* in a single year." While changes of government are never pleasant for the people being replaced, they happen in more orderly ways in Canada than in much of the world, and all of our debates, and all of our differences, rest upon a fundamental respect for the people with whom we differ. That is not the case everywhere in the world. I have been in truly divided countries, and have seen conflicts where the sides genuinely hated and feared each other. Examples abound.

When I chaired the Commonwealth Committee of Foreign Ministers on Southern Africa, I found an abiding apprehension and distrust among South Africans, white and black.

Most recently, in my work in Cyprus, on behalf of the secretary general of the United Nations, I was taken to the sites where Greek Cypriots had been killed, and then to those where Turkish Cypriots had been killed, each at the other's hands. Each side held the other principally responsible for the atrocities. Neither felt it could trust the other. Unhappily, the world is full of such stories.

But that is not the case in Canada. There is very little hatred here, very little fear. There is resentment, anger, suspicion, but those are mild emotions – you find them in every family, on every street, everywhere. More to the point, in Canada, most of those emotions are aroused by ignorance, not experience.

With occasional spectacular exceptions, the actual experiences among Canadians are good. When we meet one another, we get along, whether that is on hockey teams, or in political parties, or in the armed forces, or in the bar after a convention or a conference. In fact, that instinct to get along with others is a distinguishing characteristic of the country. It is one of the things we have in common, across our diversity and space.

And it is more than "getting along," which is an Emily Post kind of value. It is respect. We treat one another with more respect than do the citizens of many, indeed most, of the countries of the world.

Think for a moment of respect. What are the measures of a society whose citizens respect one another? Are the disadvantaged pushed out of sight, left on their own? Less in Canada than in most societies. Are people discriminated against, because of their race or colour or religion or gender? Less in Canada than in most societies. Are individuals free to develop their own talents, build their own future? Are differences respected? More in Canada than in most societies.

We are far from being a perfect society, but we are more successful than most. And much of that success is based upon a respect and a generosity which are both the opposite of and the antidote to the venoms which disable truly divided societies.

That point is important for two reasons. First, it means that there is ample common ground in Canada: the Canadian experience is that, when we get together, we get along. Indeed, the real problem is getting together, across our massive space and different languages. But that is a technical problem, just as new constitutional arrangements are a technical problem. While we will need to change the arrangements by which we live together, the country itself is not an artificial construct. There is a community here, based broadly on common values, significant shared experiences, and a fundamental respect for others.

That speaks to what we are: a genuine community, characterized by an unusual respect for differences. It also rebuts the assumption that, somehow, Canada is a failed community.

In this turbulent world, there are countries which are failing, for their own reasons, and some Canadian separatists may argue that they are analogies for Canada. That would be false. We have serious problems to resolve in Canada, but we are not a fundamentally divided community, with deeply hostile interests, unable to compromise or agree. Quite the contrary. There are communities like that in the world, and they may come apart, precisely because their divisions are much deeper than ours, and their skills of reconciliation more shallow.

The differences in Canada simply don't compare with the deep antagonisms that tear at truly divided societies. In fact, there is a profound distinction between diversity and division, and part of our considerable success as a country is that we have encouraged diversity and avoided division.

There are also federations which have failed because they were formed by force, and their component communities never did agree freely to live together. Some Canadians may be tempted to pretend that Canada is another Soviet Union, another Yugoslavia, an artificial federation bound to fail. The opposite is the truth. Those failed federations are exactly what we are not. We were formed freely, when Quebec and other communities chose to create a federation. We have functioned freely, acknowledging that members of the federation could leave if they chose, respecting different languages and needs. That is far different from federal systems where threat and force were the reasons that communities joined or stayed.

SEVENTEEN

CANADIAN GOALS

WE CANADIANS ARE SUDDENLY BEING FORCED TO FACE TWO FUNDA-mental issues. One is a question of form and process – how do we work together as a national community; who has what power, what responsibility? The more basic issue is about purpose – why should we work together, as a national community?

Most constitutional discussions have been about form. They assume some broad agreement on national purpose. But the Quebec separatist movement questions, precisely, the purpose of Canadian federalism, and concludes that a radically different arrangement would better serve the interests of their commu-nity. The rest of Canada has, by and large, been trying to answer a Quebec question about purpose with a Canadian response about form.

That should not be disparaged. Changes in purpose are often achieved by changes in form, and the most recent constitutional initiatives almost succeeded. A constitutional recognition of Quebec as a "distinct society" would have given the Quebec community more room to pursue its particular purposes.

But that particular focus took attention away from changes which have been occurring in other parts of the Canadian community, and which also raise fundamental questions about purpose. Quebec has asked those questions as a whole community. As the "distinct society," as the minority within Canada that is also the majority within Quebec, it is accustomed to thinking in terms of a whole community. That is its natural frame of reference. Other parts of the Canadian society have seen their changes as episodic, or unrelated to one another. But, over the last three decades, those changes have been profound and, often, unsettling.

Whole ways of life have disappeared. We know that intellectually, but often don't focus on what it means to individuals who have seen their worlds change, sometimes beyond recognition. That is a modern phenomenon. Through most of history, change was more gradual. Now it comes with a rush, and sweeps away the frames of reference which had provided stability and continuity before. Through most of the years of my grandfather's life, Kincardine, Ontario, where he was born, looked and felt about the same. Through most of the years of my father's life, High River, Alberta, where he was born, remained essentially the community he was raised in. Now there is a nuclear power plant at Kincardine, and the rich ranch country around High River is being infiltrated by Calgarians living on acreages, and even by factories. Moreover, satellite dishes boom blue movies into homes where, not long ago, you had to strain to get a short-wave radio signal. And the Roman Catholic Mass, which used to be in Latin, is now occasionally enlivened by guitar accompaniment. Changes like that reach beyond the physical landscape, into the psychological. They disturb the order here, and unsettle people who had come to count on that order.

This is not just something I have read about. I represented a rural constituency in Parliament for twenty-one years. Many of the people in that constituency were enthusiastic about the transformations in the modern world. They mastered the new technologies, were excited by their access to a wider world, and welcomed new immigrants, new styles, even a new morality. Some of them played guitar at Mass.

But others were threatened, suspicious, unsettled in the basic sense that they thought the moorings of their life and values were being pulled away. Those two decades brought a flood of changes which could be seen only as threatening by people who felt their values were under siege. They thought the world they knew was being steadily, even deliberately, taken away. They were unnerved, for example, by the change to the metric system, and by the false argument that the Official Languages Act would force them to speak French, and by violence that they associated with cities and immigration and, in many cases, by abortion and what they regarded as a sharp decline in moral standards. Other Canadians, including many of their neighbours, might think their reactions were extreme, but, naturally enough, that did not calm their sense of alienation.

Gradually, I saw the distress of my troubled constituents turn to anger. In some cases, I became the focus of that anger. I will never forget, on election day in 1988, visiting the polling place in Drayton Valley, west of Edmonton, and having a man in his late seventies turn on me in fury because I did not support capital punishment, which he believed would stop society's slide towards violence. It was not his view which disturbed me, but the consuming nature of his anger. He was the quintessential honest, hard-working Canadian, who had a right to be comfortable in his own country, in his old age. Instead, he was furious, and sensed himself almost dispossessed.

Capital punishment was not really the issue. To him, I symbolized a system which had betrayed the values – indeed, the country – he believed in. It was more than a personal betrayal; I was his member of Parliament, his connection to the larger community, so, in that sense, it also had let him down. I can't know how many people harbour an anger like that, but, certainly, that man in Drayton Valley was not alone. A large number of Canadians are more threatened and unsettled than they should be. This is their country too, and the community we want Canada to become must encourage a sense of belonging among Canadians who feel so threatened by the changes that have transformed every part of modern Canada.

When Maureen was growing up, near Cumberland, just east of Ottawa, the countryside south of her home town was dotted with small cheese factories. They had been part of life there for generations, and are gone now, consolidated into larger corporate operations. I have seen the same thing happen to most of the small family sawmills in Western Alberta, small fish plants on the Atlantic coast, many family-owned farms and businesses. That had a gradual, but profound, effect on rural communities in Canada, whose citizens had assumed that their world was local, and became uncomfortable when local ownership failed or fell away. Obviously, that pressure on small and family-owned enterprises wasn't just rural. When were you last in a corner store that wasn't a 7-Eleven or some similar chain?

The point is not nostalgia, but a straightforward recognition that changes in the world we know affect our attitudes and assumptions. Whatever the Canadian "sense of purpose" was when Macdonald was building his railway and Laurier was recruiting immigrants from Europe, it was intimately tied to a rural country. It stands to reason that, as the pole star which had informed that identity dimmed, the confidence in that vision of Canada would begin to erode. In many cases, no doubt, it was a good thing to wear down identities which had locked people into roles or locales which confined them. My point is simply that it was unsettling.

There has been a rush of factors that have altered the Canada we knew. Our patterns of immigration have changed sharply, to the point that we are now emphatically multiracial, with different languages, different faiths, different colours. Economic factors have changed more than the cheese factories – textile and processing and some manufacturing industries that had thrived in a smaller and more protected world, can't compete today. That has meant the closing down not just of factories, but, more important, of the assumption of security in those communities. Our mythic passenger trains have, for years, been more a symbol people cherished than a service that they used, but the failure of the symbol, when it came, also stripped away some of our sense of who we are.

In some societies, those modern changes came dramatically, sweeping old systems away, declaring a new era. Not here. No Berlin Wall came down in Canada. There was no Vietnam war, no overturning of an apartheid system. We have never been dramatic. We understate our changes as much as we do our accomplishments. Yet, in our quiet, steady fashion, the Canadian community has changed profoundly from the country of Macdonald and Cartier, and, indeed, from the country that emerged from the Second World War. No doubt Sir John would conceal his surprise, but it would be a jolt for him to step out of a time capsule today, and find neighbourhoods in Vancouver and Scarborough where Cantonese is spoken more naturally than English, and see woman judges on the Supreme Court bench, and a Métis as lieutenant-governor of Manitoba, and be told that French-speaking Canadians were running some of the largest corporations in Canada and competing aggressively in the world, and that Canadian technology was guiding satellites in space, and that per-capita income was lower in England than here in the country he had brought together.

That change in the Canadian reality begs a question about the conception of Canada, the vision we have of our country. What are the modern purposes of Canada? What are the goals which might draw us together and drive us forward? In a sense, those are very un-Canadian questions. We have not devoted much of our time to discussing matters of high national purpose. Occasionally, Canadian leaders have floated lofty invocations like "the Just Society" or "a vision of a new and greater Canada," but more usually the promise has been more pragmatic: "jobs, jobs, jobs" or that classic expression of Liberal party modesty: "King or Chaos."

Most of our accomplishments have come without much fanfare. Our federation itself was designed as a careful compromise, not a dramatic innovation. The equalization program, which assured richer and poorer regions roughly the same level of services, was regarded as being simply sensible, rather than a blow for social justice. Our tradition of respecting human rights predated the adoption of a formal charter. Canada's invention of U.N. peacekeeping was a pragmatic way to solve a problem. The result has been a country that is successful and admired, but lacks that sure sense of itself which helps comparable communities rise above their differences.

We lack that sense of ourselves in part because we have not nurtured a common understanding of what we have done together, and of the values, the history, the attitudes we share. We must do better at that, if only so that we know what we are losing before we let it slip away. However, the real issue is not what we have done together in the past but, rather, what we might do together in the future.

We have slipped into a dangerous habit of mind in this debate about Canada. We start by listing our problems, rather than our advantages, let alone our opportunities. We treat the seventh-strongest economy in the world as a burden, and our federation as some kind of ramshackle anachronism that we have to keep going because it would be an embarrassment to everyone to bring it down. That is nonsense.

For all of their understandable self-regard, none of our provinces, operating on its own, would have become as strong as it is today. And none, standing alone, has the potential that it would have as part of a larger Canada, particularly if that larger Canada uses this present opportunity to get its act together. That includes my own province of Alberta, which, before oil was discovered, struggled with poverty and welcomed the equalization payments from the rest of Canada. There is a fierce and legitimate debate about how much Alberta paid after oil was found. But whatever that sum, the modern Alberta, with its head offices and its export industries, and its reach around the world, benefits from being part of a respected, large economy and country. Would it be better off on its own, sitting between Afghanistan and Algeria in the United Nations, and sending written submissions to the G-7 Economic Summit? Would it be better off as a United State, number 51, "the one above Montana"? Alberta is rich enough that some people might say: "Well, yes . . . ," as they might about Ontario, or British Columbia, or Quebec, but not one single soul would say that about Manitoba or Saskatchewan, or anywhere in Atlantic Canada, or the North. And if the larger Canadian provinces could get along on their own, as some North American Belgium or Brunei, would they be better off? Or – if they could design their destiny – would they be better off in a Canada that had shed its doubts, and was focused on its future?

The compelling argument is not that we should stay together for yesterday's reasons, but that we should come together for the future. When we stop to think about it, the reality is that, if Canada didn't exist, we would want to invent it, because no other arrangement would serve so many of our interests so very well.

How might we turn the focus of Canadian debate from our problems to our opportunities? The most effective way would be to begin a deliberate and inclusive discussion of the goals of this modern country. We Canadians rarely talk together about goals. We discuss programs, and problems, but not purposes. We let events define our agenda, rather than trying, as other nations do, to set an agenda which can help define events.

The two dominant political issues of the last decade in Canada have been trading policy and fiscal policy. To some degree, that was the result of deliberate choices made by the Mulroney government, but, as events demonstrated, it would have been virtually impossible for any government, of any party, to ignore those priorities. When Bob Rae was elected premier in Ontario, with an NDP government and agenda, he was forced quickly to adjust to fiscal realities. When Jean Chrétien was elected prime minister, after his party had fought the 1988 election against the Free Trade Agreement and been carefully ambiguous about NAFTA, his government continued to implement both policies.

What those issues have in common is that they each required Canada to respond to forces beyond our direct control.

We are a trading nation, and our prosperity depends upon international trade more than that of the United States, or Britain, or France, or Japan. The world we were trading in changed profoundly — Europe formed its "common market"; Asian economies grew dramatically, and took markets and industries from North America; and the accelerating economies of scale meant we needed reliable markets beyond the 27 million citizens of Canada, spread across our daunting geography. There was legitimate debate about the wisdom and the details of the Canada-U.S. Free Trade Agreement, but no serious Canadian pretended we could ignore the changes in international trade.

The fiscal reality was equally relentless. Again, there was legitimate debate about how spending should be cut, and how much, but no serious Canadian pretended we could ignore the national debt.

The result was that our most basic national debates were about things we had to do, not things we wanted to do.

They were about means, not goals.

And, to many people, they were about loss, not gain — factories that were closing, job opportunities that were going to Asia, agricultural markets that were lost to European or American subsidies, military bases that were closed, government services that were reduced, hopes for child care programs that were disappointed. That sense of loss fused with a growing sense of dispossession among other Canadians who felt assaulted by the changes of the modern world, and the result was a broad atmosphere of discontent.

The formal political system was not able to respond effectively. Quite apart from a world-wide cynicism about political leadership, the Progressive Conservative government had spent most of its legitimacy by the early 1990s, and the strategy of the other parties was to help it fall, rather than propose a risky alternative. At the same time, interest groups have become more assertive, and their focus, by definition, is not upon the whole community, but upon their part of it. People think of themselves more exclusively as dairy farmers, environmentalists, Westerners, francophones, even "taxpayers," and the temptation is to see other Canadians as competitors, even antagonists, rather than as fellow citizens.

The results of the 1993 general election took some of the anger and tension out of the atmosphere, but this is still not the best climate for decisions about any nation's future. But it is the climate we have, and the way to make the most of it is to bring the whole community back into view, and have it focus upon the common purposes of Canada.

EIGHTEEN

A CHANGING
SOCIETY

BOB EDWARDS OF *THE EYE OPENER* HAD A RUNNING FEUD WITH HIS
fellow Calgarian R.B. Bennett, when Bennett was the lawyer
for the CPR. Edwards wanted the CPR to improve safety at
railway crossings in Calgary, and Bennett counselled his client
to ignore *The Eye Opener*. Edwards retaliated by running prominent pictures of wrecked trains, with a caption saying: "Another
CPR Wreck." Then he ran a picture of Bennett, and the caption
stayed the same: "Another CPR Wreck." The CPR made the
crossings safer.

With his usual subtlety, Edwards was distinguishing between
cause and effect – the effect, being the wrecks; the cause, his
neighbour in the Alberta Hotel, Bennett.

In that spirit, a small plaque should be erected at St. Pierre
de Jolys, Manitoba, because that was where it became clear that
the traditional process of constitutional discussion was a wreck.

A joint committee of the House of Commons and the Senate had scheduled public hearings of constitutional proposals for November 6, 1991. Senators arrived. So did members of Parliament, and the media – but not one single citizen. The message was clear: the normal Canadian processes of public discussion didn't work any more.

In fact, that message had been building for some time, at least in English-speaking Canada. The reaction against the Meech Lake negotiation had less to do with the contents of the agreement than with a process that was seen as manipulative and exclusive.

(To that degree, the debate about the "failure" of Meech Lake exaggerated the constitutional differences between Quebec and other Canadians. Quebecers saw the substance of Meech Lake, and approved it. Other Canadians saw the process of Meech Lake, and rejected it. As so often in Canada, the difference was of perception, not principle.)

So if the wrecks at St. Pierre de Jolys and Meech Lake are the results, what is the cause? Is there an R.B. Bennett we can blame? Or a group of R.B. Bennetts – an "élite" – whose mere removal would make things work again?

Obviously, I don't think the answer is that simple. But there is no doubt that the traditional assumptions about Canadian politics and government don't apply any more.

The danger is that people in office will simply hunker down and become defensive, and a frustrated population will be driven to nostrums that won't work.

My own view is that the major change is that more Canadians are more informed generally, and more interested in public policy, and want to have more influence upon their lives.

It's not surprising that should happen. Among our goals in Canada has been to improve education, increase leisure time, and encourage responsible citizens to think and act for themselves. That is happening, but our political institutions and practices were framed in a more authoritarian time.

For decades, we let "first ministers" decide important questions in closed meetings, where even their legislatures and Parliament had trouble intruding. For years, we have described public consultation as sending parliamentary committees out to let the public comment on agendas and proposals drawn up in Ottawa.

Those attitudes deserved to be wrecked. The challenge is to find replacements that will let the modern community of Canada solve very complicated problems.

Government is the most complex activity in our society, precisely because it must respect and balance competing legitimate forces, and move them forward together. And government is becoming more difficult, because the problems grow and the resources shrink. Yet, today, the process of government, and the profession of politics, do not themselves command the respect they need in order to lead.

Cynicism about politics is not surprising. It is natural in a democracy, and rooted in a healthy scepticism about power, and the people who wield it. Lord Acton was right: power does corrupt, and it is dangerous, in a democracy, to trust any official too completely.

But it is just as dangerous to distrust officials too completely. Scepticism should be a restraint, not a religion. Governments were not created just to hold parades and celebrations. Their basic function is to decide complex questions, on behalf of other citizens who are busy doing other things. Their responsibility is to take the time to understand the relevant issues and interests, and come to judgements that will let the whole community move forward.

Often those decisions will be controversial, involving choices among different interests, different points of view. Naturally, people who don't like the decision won't like the government.

But there is a distinction between the popularity of a specific government and the legitimacy of a system. If you trust the system, you accept decisions that go against your own interests. So, particularly in a democracy, the political system simply cannot function without a basic level of public trust.

It is always difficult to balance scepticism and trust. An attempt at that balance is at the heart of our parliamentary system. That is why we have a "Loyal Opposition," which has a double responsibility – to be loyal to the Canadian system of government, yet to be sceptical of the government of the day and the measures it proposes.

Sometimes that balance has not held. In 1982, several members of my own party, in Parliament, were so opposed to the Trudeau constitutional changes that they stormed the chair of the Speaker of the House of Commons after she ruled in favour of the government. Years later, Liberal senators used their appointed majority in the Upper House to reverse the decision of the elected House of Commons on the Goods and Services Tax.

But those were remarkable exceptions, not at all the rule. I served twenty-one years in Parliament, through several controversies, and those were the only times that anger or partisanship threatened seriously to override the rules. By and large, that arrangement in Parliament carried Canada through serious and divisive controversies, and the legitimacy of our political system remained intact.

I fear that is changing today. For one thing, public scepticism focuses on the political system itself, not just on particular politicians or proposals. For another, there is a growing disdain for the ideas of compromise and the accommodation of other interests, both of which are central to politics in all democracies, and are precisely the qualities which allowed Canada to come together in the first place, and to work successfully for 127 years.

Unquestionably, a lot of the disrespect for politics has been earned by politicians, at various levels, who, in some cases, acted improperly, or, more often, were too ready to ignore responsibility or manipulate voters. Just as clearly, some politicians who were out of office, and trying to get in, attacked the system excessively, to get at its incumbents.

The growing influence of single-issue interest groups – environmentalists, anti-tax activists, anti-abortionists, whatever – has eroded the instinct to compromise, which holds most diverse communities together. There is nothing new about any of that, but the cumulative impact threatens to immobilize Canadian political skills at a time when we need them more than ever.

There is one sense in which the Canadian political system is more vulnerable than that in comparable countries. Americans can excoriate Mr. Clinton and the Congress and still snap to attention for "The Star-Spangled Banner." The French can revile Mr. Mitterrand, and take the country out on strike, but leave their own sense of national superiority absolutely undiminished.

This is where, for Canada, the issues of legitimacy and identity intersect. There is no powerful sense of Canadian community to withstand the withering forces of frustration and cynicism.

The anti-government, anti-politician anger is no passing distemper, and it cannot be cured by palliative gestures. It reflects a widening sense that there are things seriously wrong with both government and politics in our country, and a view, one that is relatively new in Canada, that government itself is the problem.

It is interesting, and encouraging, that the anger on the

outside of government is matched by a frustration on the inside. For ten years, I worked with extremely able public servants – some of them elected, many of them career – and the best of them were frustrated by the failures of the system, knowledge-able about why it failed and how it could succeed, and ready to change things.

It has become customary to speak of élites, so let me char-acterize the referendum, and the 1993 election, as messages *to* the élites, and the growing frustration among people in gov-ernment as messages *from* the élites.

The first message is about accountability, access, being part of the system. The second message is about effectiveness, about solving problems – economic, international, constitutional, social – which may be the most challenging we have ever faced.

We have to heed both messages together. We have to be accountable and effective and, because this is Canada, we have to do that across the second-largest territory in the world, with a society whose storied diversity is edging in places into antag-onism, while carrying the burdens of debt, unemployment, and a world that is both more competitive than we have known and less stable than we had hoped.

I think that can be done, with enough goodwill and imagi-nation. The basic Canadian idea is right – the pragmatic, demo-cratic idea of respecting different forces and finding ways to advance them together. In fact, that idea – that genuine reliance on respect and compromise – is more essential to success in Canada than in other countries who are enduring their own crises of democracy.

Obviously, there is fear and anger in most modern democ-racies. Recent polls show that large numbers of the citizens of the United Kingdom wished they lived in some other country.

An anti-system candidate like Ross Perot wins millions of presidential votes in the United States. Established regimes in Japan, France, Britain, and Italy are reeling or rejected.

The interesting question is why. Many of the causes are particular to the country where they occur. Certainly that is true in Canada, where discontent can be traced back to specific issues – the National Energy Program, the Goods and Services Tax, the Meech Lake Accord, the failure of the Meech Lake Accord, free trade, patronage, the prime minister asking: "Why should I sell your wheat?"

Another factor has been the burst of problems that seem insoluble in any country – slow economic growth, disagreement on trade rules, antagonism to newcomers, terrible bloody wars, natural disasters, whether in the cod stock or the ozone layer.

Just a few years ago, when the Berlin Wall came down and the Gulf War was being prosecuted under U.N. auspices, governments seemed more in control of events. Everywhere, there is a different impression now.

But perhaps the most important new factor, in Canada at least, is the expectation by individual citizens that they will play a larger part in the decisions which affect them.

For a long time, we used to assume that most people had better things to do than worry about government or politics. I remember accompanying Robert Stanfield to a public meeting in Victoria, one warm spring evening in the late 1960s. As we drew near the school, I noticed there were not many cars in the parking lot, but plenty of people working in their gardens.

You have to break these things gently to political leaders, so I said: "It's a lovely evening. We might not have too many people at our meeting tonight." And he replied: "Isn't it comforting to know that so many people in Victoria have their priorities right?"

That was the era of "the Just Society," "the Great Society," the politics of hope and affluence. Two turbulent decades have passed, leaving debt and doubt in their wake.

But those were also decades in which more people went to school; more women were treated with more equality; more "new" Canadians reached beyond the barriers that held them back; more information rolled into our lives, from television, and computers, and the changes we found in our neighbourhoods.

Today, more people know more, hear more, see more, say more, and show more confidence in their own judgement, and less deference to others. That includes whole categories of people – notably women, but also members of cultural minorities – who had once accepted a marginal role in society, and now do not.

So we are dealing with a complex cultural change that puts immense pressure on our political institutions.

The temptation, always, is to prescribe some simple solution – hold a referendum, or balance the books. Those prescriptions may cure some disease, but they will not produce the kind of political reform that will make this country work, or keep it whole.

We need two qualities together – a system that is trusted, and a system that works. There is not much point in having a system that is so responsive it cannot lead. That would be particularly dangerous in this country.

There was no General MacArthur here, no Four-Power Agreement and no Marshall Plan, no revolution – as in the United States – and no history of battles won – as in Europe. We are a nation by agreement. That is how we started, how we function, how we succeed or fail. We have counted, more than most, on our political leaders and our political institutions, which are now in disrepute. That is no small problem.

That problem, by the way, would be no less acute in some new Canada, either without Quebec, or with Quebec on radically different terms. We delude ourselves by talking about Canada outside Quebec as though it is homogeneous, or by pretending that any arrangement with a separate Quebec would be easy. Whatever happens, we are going to need political institutions that are trusted enough, and effective enough, to see us through grave challenges.

Many of the nostrums that are proposed now — referenda, or the power to petition for the "recall" of any elected official whose actions are found offensive by electors, or a legislated limitation on the number of terms an individual can serve in public office — are simply irrelevant to Canada's real needs. They are founded upon distrust of the very institutions we have to make trustworthy. They are new ways of saying "No" when the inescapable reality is that we need new ways of saying "Yes" together — not as West against East, or wealthy against needy, or WASP against Asian Canadian. Those are differences we have to bridge together, or we will simply, as Sir John A. Macdonald said, sink into insignificance.

Looking back, I think there is a direct connection between the wreck at St. Pierre de Jolys and the success of the negotiation of the Charlottetown Accord.

I had insisted on a wide-ranging process of public hearings. Many members of the committee thought the schedule I wanted was too ambitious, given the complexity of the proposal and the deadlines for a report. Most Quebec members thought the elaborate hearing process was bizarre, because there was little interest in hearings in Quebec.

I believed we had no chance of bringing English Canada to a constitutional agreement without the most open process possible. There was a deep and lethal antagonism to the closed manipulative image of the Meech Lake process, and we had to prove that this approach was different.

Now, my "open process" had just collapsed, and I didn't know what to do.

The Special Joint Committee could continue its work, and consult specialized witnesses, but that would not provide the public participation which I believed was essential. My own government couldn't sponsor hearings on its own, because our credibility was doubly impaired – by our leadership of the Meech Lake process, and by the suspicion, with a federal election looming, that we would use the conferences for partisan advantage.

I asked advice, and B.C. premier Mike Harcourt offered an important distinction. He said: "It may be that the era of people wanting to actually go to meetings in the Legion Hall is over. What they really want now is to know that people like them will have the chance to be heard."

That turned out to be the principle we followed in the five public constitutional conferences that were held, on consecutive weekends, in Halifax, Calgary, Montreal, Toronto, and Vancouver, and the special conference on aboriginal issues held later in Ottawa. The first five conferences were co-sponsored by the Government of Canada and five Canadian public policy institutes: the Atlantic Provinces Economic Council; the Canada West Foundation; the C.D. Howe Institute; the Institute of Research on Public Policy; and the Niagara Institute.

Arthur Kroeger, one of Canada's best public servants, coordinated the process, with uncommon patience and skill. The British television series *Yes, Prime Minister* has created a caricature of senior public servants, who are portrayed as serving their own interest above all, and deploying a practised deference that leads to the easy manipulation of ministers. There are some Canadian public servants whom that caricature fits but, in my experience, not many. Certainly the team that Arthur Kroeger led showed the kind of ingenuity, dedication, and responsibility that any organization, anywhere, would envy.

What would be particularly interesting to *Yes, Prime Minister* was the way Mr. Kroeger worked with me, as his minister. His job was unusual, if not unique: these conferences, after all, had their roots in the government's loss of legitimacy, and would work only if real leadership came from the sponsoring public-policy organizations. Yet Mr. Kroeger, the government official, had to coordinate those five separate agencies, organize bilingual and multitopic conferences, in five different cities, under nearly impossible time pressures, and, at the same time, respect his responsibility to his minister. He exercised his judgement to keep me completely away from some questions, such as the actual selection of the "ordinary Canadians" who applied to participate, and to keep me fully informed about decisions that might divide the parties I needed to bring together. And then, in Vancouver, at the end of the planned series of conferences, when he was worn out and suffering from a heavy cold, I told him we needed to organize an unexpected sixth conference, on aboriginal issues. He had always been frank with me, and he said: "Mr. Minister, we cannot do that. It is not physically possible." Then he took a deep breath, and added: "But we will do it."

However, what really made the conferences work were two factors from outside government.

The first was the insistence of the policy institutes, led by the Canada West Foundation, that participation in the conferences go beyond the usual suspects, and include citizens drawn from the public at large. Advertisements in newspapers across

Canada invited Canadians to apply to participate, explaining in their applications why they thought they were qualified to discuss their country's constitution. There was a strong response and, on average, one in four participants in each conference was a member of the general public.

Those "ordinary Canadians" themselves were the other factor which made the experiment work. Their presence took the starch out of the so-called experts and authorities, and created a collegial atmosphere, which led even the most adversarial of interest groups to look for common ground. Thousands of Canadians watched the conferences live on television, and came to believe that the debate was both accessible and reasonable.

Those conferences had faults. They did not have the power to decide policy, or the responsibility to translate that policy into practice. That meant that some of the solutions that won support in a conference could not be made to work in the actual negotiation. The clearest case concerned the consensus at the Halifax conference – the first of the series of conferences, whose success gave us confidence about the new process – in favour of "asymmetrical federalism." Again, while participation at those conferences was more representative of a broad Canadian public than at any previous discussion, no one would pretend that every legitimate interest was represented or that those who were had equal weight. Anyone of a mind to find fault could, no doubt, compile a long list of things that were wrong with those conferences. But, for all their imperfections, they were a quantum move away from the secrecy and exclusiveness of the traditional constitutional process.

More than any other single factor, they created a public climate which encouraged the country's governments, when it became their turn to meet, to take one another seriously, and to seek as much consensus as the conferences had shown.

That conference model responded to the new sense of efficacy in the Canadian population. It took citizens seriously, and gave them the sense that their views counted.

It also worked well in tandem with the Joint Committee of Parliament, whose members attended each conference, and whose report reflected several of the discussions there. So it was an addition to the existing system, enriching it, not replacing it, and not threatening it.

That conference model also respected the reality of interest groups in Canada, but created an expectation that those groups would reach beyond their narrow base, to find a practical consensus. The atmosphere encouraged groups which had come as advocates, and sometimes as adversaries, to suspend hostilities and look for Canadian common ground.

That model can be applied to other public issues, which need to combine genuine public participation and decision making. Undoubtedly, different models could also be effective. The principle that worked was to change the system to make use of people and energies whose frustration, on the outside, could leech legitimacy from public decisions.

NINETEEN

THE ILLUSION OF THE "HAPPY DIVORCE"

THE PROSPECTS OF KEEPING OUR COUNTRY TOGETHER ARE MORE daunting now than at any time I can remember, in part because there seems so little will to face the stark consequences of splitting Canada.

Many Canadians in Quebec assume they could keep the advantages of Canada in a separate country. Naturally separatist leaders want to encourage that comforting view. Lucien Bouchard has announced that an independent Quebec would continue to use Canada's currency, and other separatists assume they could leave the country and still keep Canada's trade agreements and the good working relations with neighbouring provinces and our social programs.

That is the illusion of the "happy divorce." Separatist leaders may be quite sincere in thinking that things would happen that easily. But I think they are dead wrong. And I say that as the quintessentially moderate "English Canadian."

Quebecers who believe they could keep what they want of Canada and leave the rest are fooling themselves, tragically. They underestimate the disappointment and the resolution with which the rest of the country would react to separation. And it is not so much their critics they misjudge, but their friends. They assume that the generosity and understanding they have found within Confederation would extend naturally to the forces which broke up the country.

That is a serious miscalculation, on two counts. First, and most obviously, English Canadians who are hostile to Quebec now, within Canada, would be relentless and unsympathetic in any negotiation of independence. They would insist on the hardest of terms, and, in the bitter aftermath of separation, they could reasonably expect strong public support.

But the more serious misjudgement is of the attitude of the Canadians who have worked so hard to respect, and accommodate, Quebec within Canada. Personally, I have been guided by two mutually sustaining ideals, and I suspect others have motivations very similar to my own. Obviously, we believe in the integrity and vitality of the Quebec society. We admire that society, and many of us have put careers on the line to help it thrive within Canada.

But we also believe in a larger concept, a Canada of mutual respect, whose citizens will reach as far as they can to maintain a broad and inclusive community.

I understand the argument that, often, the larger Canadian community has not seemed generous to Quebec; but I also know, firsthand, how many Canadians are profoundly committed to the flourishing of Quebec within Canada. Personally, I have no doubt that, if the country is given a chance, that commitment would lead to appropriate constitutional guarantees.

Again, speaking personally, I would regard a vote to separate now as a rejection of that Canadian ideal – not just a rejection of the geographic Canada, but of the idea of the larger, more generous, community. It would be a deliberate decision to turn inward, rather than to reach out.

The issue once was whether Canadians would respect the right of Quebec to leave, if it made that choice. The clear answer is yes. The more pertinent question now is whether Quebecers will respect their responsibility to consider that option with the greatest of care, and to exercise it only as a last resort. The decision to separate would be treated by the rest of Canada as being as unequivocal as the right to make it; it would be final, and we would turn our energies to making the most of the Canada that remained.

In September 1991, my friend and parliamentary secretary, Jean Guy Hudon, arranged a public meeting for me in his home town of Valleyfield, just outside Montreal. There was a large crowd, including a good-natured handful of *indépendantistes*, who went through the motions of trying to chant me down, and then listened politely to my High River French. In the public discussion afterwards, one of my hecklers came to the microphone and said that he didn't like my constitutional proposals, or my politics, or, really, my country, but "We respect you, Mr. Clark, and we hope that, after independence, you will be Canada's ambassador to Quebec."

No one in Quebec should harbour illusions like that. If Quebec decides to leave, then the Canadians sent to negotiate the divorce would not be conciliators like me. More to the point, the people who have worked so hard to secure agreements, like

Meech Lake and Charlottetown, were doing that not as conciliators, but as Canadians; not as ambassadors, but as fellow citizens. No doubt we would retain a deep affection for Quebec, but it would then be another country, which had placed its interests in conflict with our own.

There is as much wishful thinking about the consequences of the separatist campaign outside Quebec as there is within the province. Many Canadians in other provinces either dismiss the prospect of separation or pretend that it would cost more to embrace Quebec than to break the federation.

And, as the so-called national debate drones into its fourth decade, the sides grow more distant from one another, and more distracted by other worries. The debt and the deficit dominate public discussion, skewing every issue to a bookkeeper's perspective and nourishing a sense that the present system doesn't work and, consequently, that half-examined alternatives can't be much worse. Western Canadians focus on their own sense of alienation, which is real, and unconsciously construct a zero-sum game, where a gain for Quebec must be a loss for the West, and vice versa. Aboriginal leaders, who took more risks than anyone else in the Charlottetown negotiations, and were rejected, by their own people as well, insist on the primacy of the aboriginal case. Interest groups, in an era of fiscal restraint and fundamental change, feel threatened as rarely before, and look to their own interests first.

Meanwhile, psychologically Quebec becomes more a separate society every day, differentiated from the rest of Canada as much by experience and purpose as by language. The "news" is different in French and English Canada. Major, or international, events may be covered roughly the same way on English-language television as they are on Radio-Canada and TVA, but the local stories and perspectives have very little in common. They literally report different worlds. As a consequence, English-speaking Canadians rarely see the Quebec that is televised to francophones each night. And the reverse is true in Quebec.

A friend from Quebec who served with me in Ottawa, a determined federalist, had developed the practice, when he was in Parliament, of watching CTV's *Canada AM* each morning, to keep him in some touch with developments and perspectives in English-speaking Canada. For the first few weeks after he left Parliament, he continued that practice in Quebec. Gradually he fell out of the habit, and became absorbed in his own community. Now he laments that he has no regular contact with the rest of the country. And he is a federalist, with friends and interests across Canada.

Naturally, the Bloc and Parti Québécois exploit that sense of separateness in Quebec. The last federal election gave Lucien Bouchard the gift of the prerogatives of Leader of Her Majesty's Loyal Opposition, and he is using that office to advance his cause. There may be irony in the "Loyal Opposition" working to end the country, but irony is no stranger to Canada, and Mr. Bouchard is within his rights in using the office he won. I expect we will see more trips abroad, to countries prepared to let his Canadian title be used to add credibility to the image of a separatist Quebec acting on its own in the world.

The more telling part of his strategy is the one he will use at home in Canada, particularly outside Quebec. It should surprise no one that Mr. Bouchard will undertake a program of gentle, but deliberate, provocation of other Canadians. It serves his interests to appear to reach out to the rest of the country, and serves them even more when he can inspire a response that appears impolite, or unfriendly to Quebec. Every harsh or ill-considered response is grist to the separatist mill in Quebec. The thesis Mr. Bouchard wants to advance is that the country does not belong together; whether or not a divorce would be happy, it serves the separatist interest to make divorce appear inevitable.

As a step in that direction, it would also satisfy separatist strategists if other Canadians became more engaged in what is described as "thinking the unthinkable," spinning out hypotheses about how Canada might function without Quebec. I understand the various frustrations that lead other Canadians to consider those scenarios, and the prudent argument that it is always sensible to plan for contingencies. But that draws us nearer the realm of self-fulfilling prophecy. Energies that should be turned to renewing the country would be diverted to considering alternatives. Quebecers whose faith in federalism is based on a sense that Canada can be made to work would wonder whether the rest of the country wants it to work. The political temptation would grow, in Western Canada and rural Ontario, to exploit antagonism to Quebec by appearing to advocate "alternatives." The one certainty is that, whenever other Canadians consider a divorce from Quebec, in whatever terms, Mr. Bouchard and Mr. Parizeau will be pleased.

TWENTY

CANADA IS
EVERYBODY'S BUSINESS

SEPARATISM IS NOT ABOUT ECONOMICS. LEADERS OF THE BLOC AND
Parti Québécois may have programs, or hopes, for economic
development, but their principal motivation is political and cultural. That is not to suggest they are indifferent to economic
questions, or naïve about them. Mr. Parizeau himself is a
respected economist, and the separatist movement has won
increasing support in the Quebec business community, and
among other Quebecers who take the economy seriously.

But, the motivation is very different. In most of Europe and
North America, in this age of deficits and competitiveness, economists and business people usually enter politics to have governments focus on "the bottom line." Their purpose is to have
economic realities constrain political ambition; with Quebec
separatists, the political goal is paramount, and the purpose of
the economic expertise is not to constrain it, but to make it

work in a complicated world. That is a significant difference.

The earlier phrase "sovereignty-association" is instructive; "sovereignty," a political concept, was the goal, and "association," a practical economic necessity, was the means to achieve it. But the political goal came first then, and comes first now. If we are to persuade Quebecers to stay in Canada, there must be political changes, constitutional changes, which give them confidence in a renewed federation. Economic arguments alone won't prove persuasive.

But neither can there be a decision about separation without an honest consideration of the costs. You can't tear anything apart without hurting – not a marriage, not a friendship, not an organization. And certainly there would be costs – economic, political, psychological, personal – to breaking up an economy and a country that have been closely linked together through the lives of five generations of Canadians. Naturally, there will be genuine differences of opinion about specific issues, but no honest person can pretend that we could separate Canada without costs.

That being so, we should identify those costs as calmly and honestly as possible. That imposes an obligation of restraint on people like me, who defend the idea of Canadian federalism. We should not exaggerate the advantages of staying, or the disadvantages of leaving, or the prospects of changing and renewing the Canadian federation.

But neither should our arguments be dismissed as "scare tactics" simply because they come from federalists, or from outside Quebec. Separatists who started this debate, by proposing to have Quebec leave Canada, cannot now tell the rest of us to go away and mind our own business. Canada *is* my business.

The issues reach far beyond Quebec. As the economist John McCallum put it: "The rest of Canada and Quebec are hopelessly entangled by some $100 billion in bilateral trade, a joint debt exceeding $450 billion, joint assets of substantial but unknown value, a common currency, and two centuries of common rules, institutions and legislation." That was put together by both sides; when there is a proposal to take it apart, both sides have a clear right to be heard.

What is more sensitive is that separation would challenge directly some of the most fundamental interests of other Canadians, including those aboriginal Canadians who claim title to some of the territory which Quebec considers its own. That is a dimension of the debate which some separatist leaders would prefer not to face. Speaking personally, I, too, would rather leave those questions to the courts, or to quiet negotiation, because public discussion can become quickly and deeply divisive.

But the issue of aboriginal claims is raised squarely by any proposal to take Quebec out of Canada. In good conscience, the people who triggered these most fundamental questions about Canada cannot now limit the discussion to the topics they find convenient.

Quebecers have a right to be fully informed about the implications of separation – the benefits and the costs. They should not be cut off from the arguments of either side.

My own purpose is not to scare people about separatism, or fool them about federalism, but to tell them the truth, as I see it. They have every right to reject my views, but they should be encouraged to hear them, and to hear from other federalists, as they prepare to make life-and-death decisions about Canada. If we truly respect democracy, we will want people to be able to assess the consequences of a decision before it is taken, rather than be surprised later.

This is very sensitive. Many Quebec separatists believe they lost the 1980 referendum unfairly, because of a propaganda campaign from Ottawa. Their view is that the separatists fought by the rules, and the Ottawa federalists did not. Throughout the 1991-92 negotiations, there was a constant suspicion that the federal government would not pursue real reforms, but would revert to a propaganda and publicity campaign. That interpretation of the 1980 referendum campaign casts a long shadow, and, of course, can be used to justify arguments whose real purpose is to limit, or distort, the debate in Quebec. It is easy for serious arguments to be misunderstood, and, to some degree, it is inevitable.

The answer is: be accurate and be careful, but not silent. Canadians recognize exaggeration. They recognize threats. My own view is that, on the question of Canada's future, people who threaten or exaggerate will hurt their own cause.

But Canadians who have thought seriously about this issue have a right to make their case. More to the point, Canadians, in Quebec as in Alberta, have a right to hear a calm and honest discussion, so they can make informed decisions.

I refer deliberately to Albertans, and other Canadians, as well as Quebecers. Because we all have decisions to make about Canada. Quebec has formal decisions, in a provincial election, and, perhaps, in another referendum. In one sense, that is Quebec's business. But Canada is the business of 27 million of our fellow citizens who have a direct stake in any proposal to take Canada apart.

The costs of separation would not be limited to Quebec. In fact, the costs may well be higher for Canadians living in New Brunswick, Nova Scotia, Prince Edward Island, and Newfoundland. But there would be costs everywhere in Canada, and they should be considered everywhere, in all our provinces and territories.

TWENTY-ONE

WHAT WOULD HAPPEN WITH SEPARATION?

THE ARGUMENTS URGING QUEBEC TO CONSIDER SEPARATION HAVE been made forcefully. At the other end of the debate, some Western Canadians assume that their region would suffer the least from a break-up of Canada, and may even benefit. That view is rooted in the belief that the status quo so weighs against the West that any change may be for the better. But, if there are advantages, in any part of Canada, there are also costs, in every part of Canada.

What would it cost to break up Canada? Who would gain, who would lose, and how? What would the effect be on New Brunswick, on Ontario, on Saskatchewan, not to mention on Quebec? I want to approach these questions in the most straight-forward way possible. I am not going to suggest disaster scenarios, or presume to predict dollar costs, or try to gauge psychological consequences. But separation would mean a sharp change in the life of every Canadian – as much in Atlantic Canada and Ontario and the West and the North as in Quebec itself. Following are five tangible areas where the impact would have to be considered carefully.

1. How Would the Debt be Divided?

Estimates of the debt burden Quebec could assume range widely. At the low end of the scale, Quebec's Bélanger-Campeau Commission estimates Quebec should assume about one-sixth of Canada's total national debt, or some $66 billion. At the high end, an assessment taking account of "historical benefits" would have Quebec assume one-third of the total Canadian debt, or some $128 billion. That is a lot of money, either way. Fights about money are always difficult, and when there is a $60 billion difference about who owes that, and the burden will fall on future generations, there is a virtual guarantee that any negotiation about shares of the national debt would be bitter, and would leave lasting scars.

Of course, the debt is a heavy burden for all Canadians now. But today, we hold that debt together, as one large country, established and respected in the international economy.

Would the debt burden be heavier if we held it separately? To some degree, that would depend upon the negotiation, that is, whether Quebec paid closer to one-third, or closer to one-sixth.

But that is only part of the problem. The other question is: what would the attitude be of the people to whom the debt is owed? Would the separation of Canada make them feel more secure, or less so? And if they felt less secure, what would happen to the interest rates they charge? What would happen if the negotiation on debt-sharing meant that Quebec had to pay off its debt more quickly? Where would the money come from? What services would have to be cut? What would be the liquidity problem?

Those same questions could be asked of New Brunswick or Ontario, certainly of Saskatchewan and Manitoba. Separation would mean the end of the Canada that is familiar to international capital markets. Naturally, there would be speculation that the federation would continue to unravel. What effect would that have on interest rates, and credit ratings, in the Canada that remained after separation?

There is an additional complication for the rest of Canada. Whatever agreement might be reached about shares of the debt, it would take time to work out how that burden would be transferred, to Quebec. By whatever mechanism, Canadians will hold Quebec's debt. The creditworthiness of a sovereign Quebec and a reformulated Canada would be linked inextricably, even after a political rupture. So Canada's risk premium would be tied to Quebec's. Canadians who say, blithely: "Let Quebec go. It's no skin off my nose" could wake up to find that the province was gone but the risk premium was not.

2. How Would Common Assets be Divided?

When the negotiators sat down to split up Canada, what value would be placed upon the St. Lawrence Seaway? Who would control it? How would it be managed? Why should Atlantic Canadians help pay for a facility that diverts traffic from their ports? Why should Western Canadians help support a facility that competes with their transportation systems?

There is an immense Canadian presence in Quebec — airports and highways that federal funds helped build, military bases, language schools, government offices, head offices of federal agencies, and the list goes on. Does anyone seriously believe those would simply be handed over to Quebec, without cost?

And, of course, there are national assets in the rest of

Canada that Quebec helped pay for: airports and highways, national parks, the Canadian Wheat Board, crown corporations like the CBC, government operations like the National Energy Board, *ad infinitum.*

That speaks of physical assets. There is also the network of social programs that is made possible, in part, because the combined population and wealth of the whole country has been enough to sustain it. Could two smaller countries each sustain that level of service? Would they want to, or would the changes generated by separation inspire the dismantling of those social programs too?

What would happen to the system of equalization payments, or to unemployment insurance? Obviously, a separate Quebec would not continue to receive those payments, and that would amount to a substantial loss to individual Quebecers. In fiscal 1990-91, Quebec received a net benefit of $3 billion in transfer payments under the equalization and unemployment insurance programs. Putting aside specific payments, would the system itself survive, in a time when fiscal restraint combined with a general sense that things were coming apart? If not, what would that mean for Atlantic Canada, or Saskatchewan, or Manitoba, provinces whose budgets today depend upon equalization payments?

3. How Would International Markets Respond?
Modern financial markets move at the speed of light. Their snap decisions are triggered by simple events, without the luxury of much analysis or knowledge. If Quebec decided to leave Canada, that fact would be flashed instantly to some trader on the Tokyo exchange. That trader might not know Canada from Casablanca, but would decide that any break-up is bad news and, in an instant,

haul down international financial confidence in both Canada and Quebec.

Naturally, Canadian officials would do everything possible to avoid that snap judgement before it happened, and moderate it later. But even if they were brilliantly successful, the damage would be done, because a break-up is, automatically, a signal of trouble.

And that could be just the beginning of our problems. International financial markets don't base their judgements on good intentions; they look at results. If Canada broke up, they would look to see how quickly we picked up the pieces, and they would want to know the exact nature of the new agreements on debt, and assets, and future cooperation. They would want that information immediately and, until they had it, they would put question marks over Canada, over Quebec, over any major investment or initiative associated with Toronto or Calgary or Halifax or Montreal.

With the best will in the world, those questions would take months to negotiate and resolve, probably years. If there was not goodwill, they would take much longer.

And the reality is that international capital has other places to go. Canada, and Quebec, need those capital markets more than they need us. That is true of every part of the country as well. For example, in my own region, the resource-based industries of British Columbia and Alberta are capital-intensive. They could contemplate a double whammy, of investors delaying investment decisions while creditors reassessed the risk premiums of a sovereign Quebec and what remains of Canada.

Canadians who contemplate separation should ask themselves three basic questions about the attitude of international markets. First, how likely it is that a country which split apart would suddenly come back together to write the kind of divorce settlement that would reassure international financial markets? Second, what price would your industry or region pay, in the interim? Third, can you afford to pay it?

4. WHAT WOULD HAPPEN TO INTERNATIONAL TREATIES?

The Free Trade Agreement, and other treaties, were signed by our trading partners with a whole Canada, not two smaller parts, and our splitting up amounts to a fundamental change in the premise of the agreement. Once the agreements are reopened, we will face again, from our trading partners, pressures which the whole Canada was strong enough to resist, but which smaller entities may not be.

A related question concerns Canada's standing in international organizations. In most of those organizations, we have great influence, more than our numbers warrant. To some degree that has been attributable to our success at home, and a divorce would raise questions about that influence. We may continue to exercise it, and we may not. But, as a whole country, we could take it for granted; as something less, we could not.

There is one group where a separated Canada would lose its seat. That is the Group of Seven Economic Summit, whose other members are the United States, the United Kingdom, France, Germany, Japan, and Italy, with the European Union participating regularly. It is one of the most influential groups in the modern world, the cockpit where the economic policy of the industrialized economies is coordinated, and often set. Many countries want in to that Summit, and can't get there. For some time, because our economies are relatively smaller, there have been gentle pressures to exclude both Canada and Italy. The separation of Canada would lead inevitably to our departure from the Economic Summit.

Canada is due to host that Summit in 1995, in Halifax. The Bloc Québécois leader, Mr. Bouchard, protested that the meeting should be held in Quebec City. The city is not the issue. A separated Canada would not have to worry about hosting the Economic Summit. The choice will not be about Canadian cities, but about what countries would take Canada's place at the Summit, after we were split and gone. The real question is whether, in the future, the people who are now Canadians will be inside that Summit, as equals, or outside, as spectators.

5. WHAT CONTROL WOULD QUEBEC EXERCISE
OVER THE CURRENCY IT WOULD USE?

Separatist leaders have said an independent Quebec would use Canadian currency. That offends some other Canadians, who find it bizarre that Quebec would want to break up the country but keep Canadian currency, with its portraits of the Queen.

However, as a legal matter, there is no question that a sovereign Quebec could use any currency it chooses: the French franc, the Canadian dollar, the Japanese yen. It could simply declare that Canadian currency would be legal tender in an independent Quebec.

The only way a Canadian government could stop that would be to impose severe foreign-exchange controls upon Canadians. That would create its own havoc. For example, controls like that would mean a strict foreign-exchange allowance for every Canadian taking a vacation in Hawaii, visiting a relative in Europe or Asia, or planning a business trip to the United States.

But the real question is not the name of the currency. It is the control an independent Quebec would exercise over that currency. It is, precisely, a question of sovereignty.

The Bank of Canada issues Canadian currency and, with the government of Canada, establishes the monetary policy which affects the value of that currency.

Would an independent Quebec expect to sit on the board of the Bank of Canada? Would the rest of Canada put up with that?

Would an independent Quebec expect to participate in the setting of Canadian monetary policy? Would the rest of Canada put up with that?

By using Canadian currency, an "independent" Quebec would sharply limit its ability to make its own economic policy. For example, it could not finance government expenditures by expanding the money supply, because that power would stay with Canada.

So the only way for a separate Quebec to gain some control over its own policy would be to work in lock-step with the central bank, and the government, of the country it just left. What kind of sovereignty is that?

Hopeful separatists may argue that the rest of Canada, after adjusting to the shock of separation, would agree to some reasonable form of monetary union. That might be true, or it might not be; no one can predict how conciliatory, or angry, other Canadians might be after separation.

Two things, however, are clear. First, an independent Quebec would have no power to force a decision on a monetary union. That would be up to Canada. Second, any arrangement that might be made on monetary policy would be dominated by the majority population, which is in the rest of Canada.

These monetary and currency questions would also raise major problems for the rest of Canada.

For the sake of argument, assume there is so much bitterness that Quebec is driven to a separate currency. Today, trade between Quebec and the rest of Canada amounts to $100 billion each year. There are plenty of complications, but currency is not one of them. If that trade were conducted in separate currencies, the transaction costs alone are estimated to be $1 billion, in 1991 dollars. It would create yet another non-trade barrier. Questions would arise as to how Quebec's share of the national debt would be denominated, and whether Quebec would market debt in its own currency.

Most critically, a separate Quebec currency would impose real exchange-rate risks on both communities. To international markets, separation would create two new countries, not one, and separate currencies would dramatize that reality. Today, political stability is an asset that Canada can take to the bank, or to the bond markets. Not so after separation, not for Quebec or Canada, not for provinces seeking investment or provinces worried about their credit rating. And separate currencies would make it worse.

Using the same currency would create different problems for the rest of Canada. It is hard enough to pursue effective monetary policy now. How much harder would it be if representatives of another country, with different needs and priorities, sat at the table? Even if no Quebecers were there, Canadian monetary policy would be far more complicated, simply because our currency would be used by another large economy, about one-third the size of our own and with a different political structure.

TWENTY-TWO

HOW WOULD OUR COMPETITORS REACT TO THE BREAK-UP OF CANADA?

WHATEVER OUR DIFFERENCES AT HOME, THERE IS ONE REALITY ON which most Canadians agree: that is, that the world we live and trade in has changed profoundly.

In fact, there is a more jarring truth: our comfortable continent is falling steadily behind our competitors, particularly in Asia.

In 1960, the economies of North America accounted for 37 per cent of what the world produced. Last year, the figure was 24 per cent, and by the year 2000, it will be down to 23 per cent. Compare that North American performance with that of just part of Asia – the economies of China, Japan, Hong Kong, Korea, Malaysia, Singapore, Taiwan, and Thailand. In 1960, they accounted for 4 per cent of global GNP; in 1992, 24 per cent; and by the year 2000, their proportion of total world production is expected to rise to between 28 and 30 per cent.

Those are extremely dynamic economies, with populations which are productive, innovative, and educated to prevail in the modern world. They are tough competition.

And they are not alone. For all of its tensions and growing pains, the European Union has transformed Europe, and made its societies and economies more modern and competitive.

Throughout Latin America, strong new trading arrangements are helping economies grow stronger, and people become better educated and more productive.

The children growing up in Canada today have to compete in that world. They have to be as well-trained as the Japanese, as innovative as the Americans, as well-organized as the Europeans.

That won't happen by accident. More than ever before, national policies will determine personal futures. The next five years will decide which societies will best prepare their children for this modern world, and which will not.

That raises two simple questions for Canadians. First, how many things can we do at once? Second, what will the rest of the world be doing while we sweat over the fine print of our divorce?

Those basic questions lead to others, which can't be ignored in any honest assessment of the consequences of separation:

Would Canada's good reputation, as a stable place to trade and invest, survive separation?

Have we the ingenuity, and the energy, to take Canada apart, and build new countries, and still keep pace with nations whose single-minded goal is to strengthen their economy or train their people?

Are the Koreans, or the Europeans, or the Americans likely to say: "Well, they have some problems up there, north of the forty-ninth parallel, so let's lay off them for a while until they get their houses in order"?

If our leaders are busy dividing up the debt, and shoring up the dollar, who will be taking initiatives to improve our schools or help our economy compete? Who will be ensuring that we take full advantage of the opportunities that are open, for Canada, around the Pacific Rim? Who will press our advantages in Latin America?

Who will have time to compete with the governments in Brussels and Seoul and Washington — and Paris — that will be aggressively seeking advantages for their countries, against all comers?

And if, for the sake of argument, our economy suffers while other economies grow, will investors put their money here, or elsewhere? If, six months after separation, an Alberta firm competes, for money or markets, with an Australian firm, who has the likely advantage?

And how does all this affect a sixteen-year-old student in Quebec or in Alberta?

TWENTY-THREE

THE COUNTRY THE
WORLD ADMIRES

THE GREAT IRONY ABOUT CANADA IS THAT, AT THE VERY MOMENT we are thinking about coming apart, the rest of the world is looking to our model.

Many poorer countries have always envied Canada, simply because we are rich. But what is happening now goes well beyond envy, and is not confined to poorer countries.

The society we have established here is judged, by most in the world, to be a success. Indeed, it is judged to be more successful than that of any other country in the world. The United Nations has begun the practice of comparing the quality of life in all of its member nations and, in 1994, once again, the U.N. declared Canada to be the best place in the world to live. Switzerland was second, Japan third, and others trailed behind.

That is not a casual judgement. It results from a careful

assessment of our economy; of our treatment of senior citizens, and women, and minorities; of our environmental standards; and of other factors. And it applies the same hard tests to Canada as it does to every member of the United Nations. Some other societies are more successful than we are on particular questions, but, overall, Canada literally leads the world.

This is not a new test, or a sudden development. That U.N. assessment began four years ago, and Canada has been judged first or second every year.

No one should be complacent about that. The judgement is not that we are a perfect society, merely that we are more successful than the others — all the others. In fact, that success is attributable precisely to the reality that we are not a complacent country, and that we seek to continue to improve the quality of Canadian life, with initiatives ranging from human-rights laws to an acid-rain treaty, to literacy programs being pursued now by ministers of the Chrétien government.

But if we should not be complacent, neither should Canadians be indifferent to the fact that our country is judged independently to be the best place in the world to live. That is not a trophy that one puts in a glass case and looks at. That is a judgement about the society in which we are living our lives — it is extremely personal to each of us, because, were we living elsewhere, our chances for quality health care, or for equal treatment before and under the law, or for clean air, would be less than they are in Canada.

U.N. assessments are one thing, but the sincerest form of flattery is when other countries try to make their systems more like ours. Consider some current examples, as fresh as today's newspaper.

The United States, no trivial society, has given its highest domestic priority to creating a health care system that is more like Canada's.

Japan, as it becomes involved in international peacekeeping, comes to Canada to learn what we do, and when it devises its enormous program of international assistance, comes to the Canadian International Development Agency for guidance.

South Africa, as it fashions judicial and political systems which might bring and keep together diverse and divided communities, calls on Canadian experts and experience.

Vietnam, as it moves from a collectivist past to a market-economy future, draws on the practical experience of Canadian *caisses populaires*.

Countries of Eastern and Central Europe, emerging from state control to free societies and market economies, seek the advice of Canadian businesses, legal authorities, teachers, and bureaucrats.

Mexico, when it seeks to enter the world trading community, comes first to Canada for advice on the GATT, and then incorporates into NAFTA principles of parity pioneered in the Canada-U.S. Free Trade Agreement.

China, conscious of the challenge of maintaining national policy in a large land of strong provinces, is very interested in Canada's federal experience.

These are contemporary national expressions of an international admiration of Canada which I found consistently during my time as secretary of state for External Affairs. Sometimes we assume that foreign admiration focuses on the physical beauty of Canada, or other factors we inherited. In fact, a lot of the admiration is of what we have done with our inheritance, an admiration of the values and skills of Canadians.

Consider some random examples.

Zimbabwe relied heavily on foreign teachers, in the long aftermath of independence, and it drew teachers from around the world. In an informal conversation, Zimbabwean education officials told a Canadian International Development Agency officer that Canadian teachers were the best who taught in Zimbabwe — better than the British, or the American, or the Zimbabwean teachers — because, consistently, they showed respect for the individual talents of the students in their classes. We don't think about it much, but, in our peaceful and diverse society, demonstrating that kind of respect for others becomes second nature to many Canadians, and shows in the way we work in the world.

I led the Canadian delegation to the launch of the Uruguay Round of Trade Negotiations, and made an official visit to Argentina, en route. Maureen's practice was to schedule independent meetings with women's groups, when she accompanied me, and among those she met were Argentinian Mothers of the Disappeared, whose children had vanished from the streets under the previous authoritarian regime. They wanted guidance as to how they might establish a human-rights organization, and inquire into the fate of their children. Other nations, notably the United States, had offered help, but these Argentinian women made it clear that what they had heard about Canada made them more comfortable with help and advice we might offer.

The British economist and commentator Barbara Ward once called Canada "the first international country." Most Canadians are generally aware of the respected reputation of Canada in world affairs. Although, like most Canadian virtues, we understate them whenever we can. Certainly, I was reminded regularly, in my Yellowhead constituency, that the United Nations and South Africa and NATO mattered less to many Canadians than their pension cheque or the GST.

In January 1989, I brought senior officials of the Department of External Affairs to Jasper, in my constituency, for three days of planning the international initiatives and factors Canada should consider in the next four years. There was a reception, to which several Jasper citizens were invited. Derek Burney, then Canada's ambassador to the United States, got into conversation with one of my constituents and, practising his diplomacy, said: "You must be pleased that your member of Parliament is Canada's foreign minister." To which my constituent replied: "We'd be a lot better off if he were the minister of Public Works."

In fact, I suspect that many Canadians underestimate the impact of Canada internationally. On a personal level, if they have travelled abroad, they know that a Canadian passport, or a Canadian flag sewn on your backpack, will win a welcome virtually everywhere, and sometimes will open doors that would be closed to the citizens of less admired countries.

But if your window on the world is a TV screen, in this time when the cameras focus more on nations with troubles or power, you could have the sense that Canada is present, but not important. For more than fifty years, such an impression has been false – and in the years to come, with the Cold War over, the skills that Canada personifies will become even more important in international affairs.

I am writing this in early June, on the very days when the fiftieth anniversary of D-Day is being celebrated. And I am writing it near San Francisco, where, normally, the only time television commentators mention Canada is when some cold front moves down to mar another perfect day. Yet the American television references to D-Day are full of Canada, because the valour and the sacrifice of Canadian troops were central to the liberation of Europe.

Canada's role was just as decisive in defining the institutions which shaped the postwar world.

The phrase "present at the creation" is customarily used respecting the nations, including Canada, who signed the original Charter of the United Nations. But it is too passive a phrase. Canada was more than simply present, whether at the creation of the United Nations, or of the North Atlantic Treaty Organization, or of the Colombo Plan. We played an active and decisive role in shaping those historic institutions, both when they were formed and as they developed.

John Humphries, of Canada, drafted much of the International Declaration of Human Rights. Lester Pearson persisted until the United States accepted a provision for political cooperation, Article 2, which made NATO more than just a military alliance. Canada was one of the architects of the Commonwealth's Colombo Plan, which became one of the pioneering institutions in international-development assistance.

That pattern has continued, consistently, for fifty years, under Liberal and Progressive Conservative governments, majority and minority. It led to the creation of institutions like La Francophonie, practices like peacekeeping, initiatives like the Treaty on the Law of the Sea. Its characteristic has been the consistent strengthening of the multilateral process, whether the General Agreement on Tariffs and Trade, the Non-Proliferation Treaty, the Commonwealth campaign against apartheid, proposals to encourage cooperation around the Pacific Rim, or other initiatives.

That leadership in international institutions is an established Canadian practice, almost a trademark. And it has created a pattern of response by other nations.

There are lots of nation-states – 184 members of the United Nations, at last count, several with populations larger than

Canada's, some with populations smaller than Quebec's. Under U.N. rules, all those nations have a right – an equal right – to offer their views in the debates of the General Assembly. They are, technically, equal.

But some countries have much more influence than others – more than their population would warrant, or their size, or their wealth. Those are the nations to which others turn, when there are difficult problems or challenging issues. Canada – a whole Canada – is one of those countries.

Let me illustrate what that means, using examples.

The Peace Process in Cambodia

The war in Cambodia was one of the most gruesome in this century. It is a small country, strategically important, and so torn by armed and brutal factions that the prospects for peace long seemed unlikely. In 1989 a conference was convened in Paris to seek some means to build a durable peace. As the discussion proceeded, it became clear that the most difficult problem would be to get agreement on a cease-fire, and to set up international mechanisms to control and supervise any settlement. That became the mandate of "The First Committee" of the Paris Conference. Two countries were needed to chair it – one from the developing world, one from the developed; one from Asia, one from outside. Canada and India were asked to lead that process, and their work was critical in devising a way that established a reasonable peace.

The Commonwealth and Apartheid

The principal victims of apartheid were the people of South Africa. However, that issue could also have torn apart the Commonwealth as an international organization, because many

African countries wanted to adopt a position of principle too categoric for the United Kingdom to accept. The modern Commonwealth is one of the few international organizations which brings together, in a family atmosphere, countries which differ widely in their level of development, and cultural makeup, and ideology. Those differences could easily have become major faultlines during the application of intensive international pressure against apartheid. Instead of coming apart, the Commonwealth was in the vanguard of a campaign that hastened the end of apartheid. I think it true to say that Canada played the critical role – a role no one else could have played – in keeping the Commonwealth together in that process. Prime Minister Mulroney chaired a meeting of the Heads of Government of the Commonwealth, in Vancouver in 1987, which established a Committee of Foreign Ministers on Southern Africa. That committee was led by Canada, and guided a campaign which was successful both against apartheid, and in maintaining the integrity of the Commonwealth.

THE BARTON GROUP ON DISARMAMENT

During the Cold War, discussions of arms control were limited by East-West tensions, even at the United Nations Conference on Disarmament at Geneva. NATO countries met in caucus exclusively with other NATO countries, the Warsaw Pact with the Warsaw Pact, and the neutral and non-aligned nations met in a third solitude. Some informal means was needed to move the discussion of arms control out of the strict shadow of the Cold War. In 1973, other countries asked Bill Barton, Canada's ambassador for Disarmament, to convene an informal committee of democratically oriented countries that would reach beyond the NATO members. That unofficial group took

Ambassador Barton's name, and became a permanent part of the world's discussion of arms control. Usually, in the U.N. system, the chairmanship of even informal committees is rotated among countries, but not in this case. Canada was always called upon to draw the other participants together. When the Cold War ended, a successor committee, chaired by Canadian ambassador Peggy Mason, was the first political consultative group in the United Nations to break all the former Cold War barriers, drawing together countries from the three groups that used to meet in isolation – NATO, the Warsaw Pact, and the neutral and the non-aligned.

DEVELOPING COUNTRIES AND THE ECONOMIC SUMMIT

Developing countries fear that the annual Economic Summit of the "Group of Seven" major Western economies will not take enough account of their concerns. Many of those developing countries have close economic or historic connections to other members of the G-7. Yet, regularly, when they needed influence in matters on the G-7 agenda, they came to Canada for help. In 1987, when he was president of the Organization of African Unity, President Kenneth Kaunda telephoned Prime Minister Mulroney at the Summit, and as a direct result of their conversation, African concerns were discussed seriously at the Summit. When we hosted the G-7, in Toronto in 1988, I held a formal preconsultation in Montreal with ministers from Latin America.

We are neither a small country, nor a small power, but we are small enough to know the value of having agreed-upon rules and common procedures in international practice. And we are respected enough, and have enough ingenuity, to play a disproportionate role in making that system work.

While we have carried our full weight during the Cold War,

and during hot wars, we Canadians prefer an order based on agreement to one based on power. That attitude in foreign affairs reflects some lessons we learned at home. Our foreign policy does not try to recast the world in Canada's image, precisely because we have learned, in our domestic policies, not to try to impose the characteristics of one part of Canada upon other members of our diverse community. We have learned at home to combine common purpose with a genuine respect for legitimate differences.

It is an interesting question whether our international authority would survive our disintegration at home. There are two reasons to believe it would not.

The first has to do with reputation. There is absolutely no doubt that some of the authority I carried into the chair of the Commonwealth Committee on Southern Africa had to do with Canada's success in harmonizing differences at home. So much of the world's work is to find common ground among people who believe they disagree. That is precisely what Canada has done, better than most, for so long, in our own diverse community. Whatever the personal skills of our diplomats and leaders, there is no doubt that Canada's success at home contributes to our credibility and effectiveness in the world.

That was not just my experience. When Lucien Bouchard was given the opportunity, by Prime Minister Mulroney, to organize the Quebec Summit of La Francophonie, his Canadian credential counted for more of his success than his fluent French or his personal skill. When Stephen Lewis, as ambassador to the United Nations, spoke in that forum, his eloquence was compelling, but he was influential because he spoke for Canada.

There would, of course, be forums – like the Economic Summit – to which a broken Canada would not be invited. But even in the places where we kept our seat, or had two seats, our reputation would be diminished, and our representatives less influential. A successful Canada is in the front row of nations now, but we would fall back if we lost the integrity that is such a large part of our credential.

The other reason for our loss of international influence would simply be that the remnants of Canada would be smaller, and preoccupied at home. We would be seen to not have the time, or the creative energy, to make the contribution that the world has come to count on from Canada.

That would be unfortunate at any time, but particularly now. The constructive internationalism which is a Canadian trademark is more necessary than ever in a world without superpowers, because more depends upon diplomacy and mediation, and less on power and command.

The Berlin Wall divided more than Germany. It was the symbol of a world divided by ideology, in which everyone was under threat, because the balance between the so-called East and the so-called West was maintained by their mutual ability to launch a nuclear war. So, when the wall came down, there was a great sense of release, and of optimism.

That optimism was compounded by other international developments, which suggested that the change reached beyond issues directly associated with the Cold War.

For example, in South Africa, a then-new president, F.W. De Klerk, took the critical decision to release Nelson Mandela, and Mr. Mandela used his freedom, and his unparalleled moral authority, to urge moderation on his supporters.

In Latin America, which was then torn by tension between the United States and the Sandinista government of Nicaragua, the Sandinistas accepted the idea of free elections and then, when they lost the vote, respected the result.

Those events sound dry, retold at a distance. The very words "foreign policy" suggest something remote – by definition, someone else's business. But it isn't remote on this globe that has become a village. And it is full of emotion.

I chaired the committee of Commonwealth foreign ministers dealing with southern Africa. Shortly after his release from prison, Mr. Mandela wanted to demonstrate that his new freedom gave him direct access to the world. And he wanted to thank the members of the African National Congress, in exile, who had supported his cause. So he made an early, ceremonial, visit to ANC headquarters in Lusaka, the capital of Zambia.

I was privileged to be among the people who met him, on his first free steps out of South Africa, and then we sat down to discuss what would happen next in his country. Someone spoke critically of the Afrikaaners – and Nelson Mandela, who had just spent long years in an Afrikaans prison, told his peers in the ANC: "You have to understand how hard it is for them to change the attitudes of a lifetime, and to work with us as equals." I found it extraordinary that anyone could show such generosity towards his captors, and it was a dramatic symbol of the deep changes that became commonplace in the late 1980s.

Whether or not there is a "new world order," there can be no doubt that the world of 1994 is markedly different from that of 1984. One could argue that circumstances are more dangerous now than they were when the superpowers were in a nuclear face-off, if only because that face-off, while immensely threatening, kept other conflicts quiet.

There is more disorder now, and it is contagious. It leaps

across old barriers, and creates its own psychology of insecurity, exactly the opposite of what we anticipated when the old walls came down.

But the Cold War bottled up more than the tensions which have exploded so brutally, for example, in Bosnia-Herzegovina. It also held back other, more creative and constructive energies.

The "Cold War" was a phrase to take literally. If it did not exactly freeze initiatives by institutions and countries which were not superpowers, it chilled those initiatives, and did not encourage them to blossom. But, if it constrained those initiatives, it did not stop them, particularly on questions that were not in the direct sights of the superpowers.

In some cases, policy changes in individual countries had broad implications, as, for example, when Japan became a major contributor of official development assistance.

In other cases, there were significant multilateral initiatives, such as the Cairns group on trade, the Contadora process, the Commonwealth campaign on southern Africa, the strengthening of regional organizations like the Association of South East Asian Nations (ASEAN), and the Southern African Development Coordinating Conference (SADCC), and various U.N. initiatives respecting the status of women, the environment, and children.

The result is that the international community has developed a significant pool of countries and institutions talented in problem-solving. Many of those talents were in suspended animation through much of the Cold War era, and the test now will be whether they can be coordinated and applied to bring more order to this postwar world.

We should hope they can be, because the forces that kept the old order don't apply any more. One of the superpowers is gone, and the other cannot, and should not, reach everywhere.

New regional powers will doubtless arise, but their reach, and their interest, will be more limited. International organizations and arrangements will have to play a larger role, but that too will depend upon the leadership of nations who believe in multilateralism.

Canada is pre-eminent among the countries whose abilities and reputation are needed now. Not only are we skilled ourselves at the mediation and consensus the world requires, but we are respected enough to provide leadership to others who share our talents. We have entered an era where, if Canada stays together, we would have an unparalleled opportunity to influence international events.

TWENTY-FOUR

THE UNKNOWN
COUNTRY

FIFTY YEARS AGO, BRUCE HUTCHISON WROTE ABOUT CANADA, FOR Canadians, in a book entitled *The Unknown Country*. Today, after decades of history lessons, books, television specials, and revolutions in the means of communication, the title holds. To most of its citizens, Canada is still an unknown country.

Why is that the case?

I believe there are three related reasons.

The first is that Canadians are not taught enough about Canadian history. Joseph Howe, the great Nova Scotian of Confederation, urged his compatriots to "boast about your country," and his advice is widely ignored. It may be that boasting has itself become an "un-Canadian activity." But, what is more remarkable, is that no consistent effort is made even to learn about the country.

While comparable nations rear their children on stories of the best of their past – from the glory that was Greece to the

Empire on which the sun never set, to the French Revolution, to the Declaration of Independence – we Canadians usually treat our history as though it didn't happen.

In part, that is because we sit next to a nation that is a communications colossus, which can spin its stories, in the language most of us speak, relentlessly into our consciousness. That phenomenom erodes national cultures eveyrwhere, from Japan to Djhibouti, but the influence is inescapable in the North American society next door. Some years ago, Maureen wrote a book describing the Canadian parliamentary system to young Canadians, and she was invited to discuss the book with students at a school in the heart of Toronto, in a neighbourhood where many new Canadians lived. The students were inquisitive and intelligent, but the television they saw, and the news they heard, the news in Canada, had not prepared them for parliaments or prime ministers, let alone a governor general. They knew about the president, and thought we had one. In the summer of 1994, they would know about Wyatt Earp and O.J. Simpson. At various times, Canadian policy has tried to block that American influence, but that pursuit is increasingly futile, so the question is: how do we offset it? As Maureen found with her book, the problem is not simply to have our own stories told, but to have them register.

There is no doubt that that has become more difficult with the slipping away of some of the symbols we regarded as particularly Canadian. Again, the most dramatic case was the railway, which was celebrated long after it stopped being used. I was part of a national government which cut back rail service in Canada, and we moved slowly and reluctantly. But I, for one, became convinced that we could not justify the cost of transcontinental trains which people wouldn't ride. Some other Canadians believe that the free-trade agreements, or the privatization of crown corporations like Petro-Canada, cost us too much in terms of national identity. What is beyond question is that national symbols are important, but, everywhere, are more difficult to sustain in a wide open world.

In February 1992, Graham Fraser, writing in *The Globe and Mail*, compared textbooks used in Quebec and Saskatchewan schools to teach high school students the history of their country. The Saskatchewan text, *Roots of Society*, contained only three references to Quebec; the Quebec text, *Le Québec: héritages et projets*, had only one reference to Saskatchewan. And those passing references told virtually nothing about the culture or society of the other Canadian province. Saskatchewan was referred to as a place where many Métis went; the Quebec references were to the roots of the Civil Code and French Canada's rejection of the American Revolution. Generally speaking, the two texts were not about the same history, so it is not surprising that adults, emerging from those schools, would have a very skewed view of their country, and little sense of holding anything in common. Fraser quotes Esther Demers, one of the co-authors of the Quebec textbook, as saying the curriculum guidelines of the Quebec Department of Education stipulated a focus on Quebec. Although guidelines in some other provinces convey a broader perspective, the textbooks on Canadian history vary from province to province, so there is no common story of the country.

Obviously, textbooks are only one source of young Canadians' sense of their country. Most teachers supplement the formal texts, and television has transformed the context within which students learn. But we pay a very high price for a system where what you know of your country depends so completely on where you were taught its history.

I have been in several schools, across the country, where teachers consciously correct those narrow perspectives on the country. In those schools, and many I haven't been privileged to visit, an extraordinary effort is made to teach the whole history of this unusual country and to impart some appreciation of the nature of our complex and accomplished nation. I have met with senior high school students who have ploughed through the Confederation debates, know the names and the routes of the Canadian explorers, and regularly read newspapers and magazines from different parts of Canada, in French, in English, and sometimes in other languages. Their schooling immerses them in Canada, and they are both enthusiastic and exacting about their country.

I say "exacting" because, in the best of those schools, students regularly tested the premises of the arguments I brought before them, and rarely sought refuge in simple patriotism when they talked about their country. On the contrary: I remember vividly a Scarborough student, in a multischool assembly, who heard me propose that we should show more pride in Canada – "wave our flag a little more" – and who stood to warn me: "Be careful about that. We don't want to be like them." – pointing south – "We have to be who we are."

He is absolutely right. But to be who we are, we have to know who we are, and that is where something in our system fails. It is too simple to blame the schools; those classes that teach the whole Canada, even though they are probably the exceptions, prove that many schools take extremely seriously their duty to teach about Canada. Moreover, and most important, they prove that Canada is a subject Canadian students can find compelling.

However, I have also been in other Canadian schools, where the questions and observations of the students did not suggest that much priority was given to teaching about Canada. Too often, those discussions fed back, undiluted and fully digested, the opinions of local hot-line commentators, or the prejudices of parents. There was not much evidence of debate, or curiosity, or even a sense that the country mattered much.

I suspect that teachers in Quebec who sympathize with separatism do not teach much about the large Canada I have come to respect. Similarly, I would not be surprised if some teachers in Western Canada offer a selective and sceptical version of the history of Quebec, and perhaps of Canada as a whole.

So, if we are serious about keeping and building a large Canada, we must encourage more schools to teach more facts about the history and nature of our country. It should not be propaganda, because that is not who we are. But it should tell the Canadian story honestly, and reasonably fully, and in the same way in every part of Canada. That will help young Canadians know what they are part of, and prepare them better, if the time comes, to judge whether the Canadian community is worth keeping.

The second reason we are such an unknown country to ourselves is that something in our nature does not like neat and dramatic myths. This country would have driven John Phillip Sousa to distraction. He was the band-master, the composer of marches, who wove tales of American conquest into martial music. By and large, Canada's history has been the opposite of conquest. The people of this country have plenty of courage and strength, as we have demonstrated amply in world wars and in building a nation against the harsh elements of nature. But, given a dispute, our instinct is to settle, while the instinct of many others is to fight.

That pragmatism, that peacefulness, has been a pattern

throughout our history. Comparisons between different societies are always inexact, but it is true that, at the very time the United States was torn by a civil war between its two principal communities, the Canadian Confederation brought our two different cultures together, peacefully, by political agreement. Again, both North American nations were drawn westward, by vast territory and new frontiers, but the settlement of the western United States was marked by violence, and the settlement of the Canadian West was not. The writer Wallace Stegner lived in both Wests, and his book *Wolf Willow* recounts the brief life, and unusual death, of a man named Marmaduke Graburn, a member of the North-West Mounted Police.

In 1879 he was nineteen years old, a rookie sub-constable recently recruited in Ottawa, a boy with an itch for adventure and a name that might have come from a Victorian novel. Graburn Coulee, back of Fort Walsh a few miles, is the name the maps now give to the draw where he rode alone after an axe he had left behind, and was followed and shot in the back of the head by Star Child, a Blood Indian with a grudge. He died alone and uselessly. . . . He was not the first Mountie to die on the job. Others had died of fever, or gone under in the quicksand of rivers, but he was the first to die by violence. In their first five years, from the beginning of the march from Fort Dufferin to the time when Star Child raised his sawed-off fusee behind the unsuspecting boy in an aspen-whispering coulee in 1879, the Mounted Police had neither killed nor been killed. Merely by the unusualness of his death, young Graburn demonstrated the quality of the force to which he belonged. They had come to the Cypress Hills in 1875 to smother a hornets' nest. In 1883 they left the Hills pacified and safe. . . .

An instinct for cooperation emerged regularly as Canadians built their new country, forming credit unions and co-operatives and farm unions throughout English-speaking Canada, and the *caisse populaire* movement in Quebec. New frontiers were settled by families, or church or ethnic groups, which functioned as whole communities, working together. When the need arose, Canadians formed public enterprises – Ontario Hydro, the Alberta Treasury Branches, and the large family of national crown corporations – to achieve common purposes.

Members of our armed forces fought with distinction in two world wars, and in the Korean conflict, and then our military won even wider admiration by its skill at keeping peace.

Those qualities of conciliation, tolerance, understanding, and compromise are genuine characteristics of the national community that is Canada. They recur through our history, and distinguish us from other countries. But they are quiet qualities. They don't translate easily into the kind of national myth, or identity, that can reach across great distances and differences. How do you write stirring marches about keeping peace? How do the prosaic purposes of our constitution – "peace, order and good government" – compete on an applause meter with the French invocation of "Liberté, égalité, fraternité" or the self-absorbed certainty of Americans who "hold these truths to be self-evident"?

Part of our fate is that the quiet qualities that characterize Canada can easily be taken for granted. That is the third reason why Canada is such an unknown country to so many of its citizens. Because we know so little of how our community came to be, because its qualities are not strident or "in our face," we assume that the benefits of Canada came effortlessly, that they will endure whatever we might do, that they are part of a birthright. From that premise, it is easy to move a step beyond taking the country for granted and assume that what we have achieved — our individual prosperity, our strength as a province, our security in asserting our "rights," our standing when we go abroad — is our own accomplishment, and has little to do with Canada.

I have referred before, in this text, to the U.N.'s judgement that Canada is a better place to live than any other country. What truly surprises me about that assessment is how many Canadians rush to dispute it. Some point out, correctly, that, while Canada is judged best overall, there are specific categories where we rank behind some other country. Others argue that the U.N. criteria are faulty, or that they don't take account of all the relevant factors. If Canada were a hockey team, and won the Stanley Cup, we would insist that there was some mistake, that the goal judge was blind, or the other team was unfairly penalized. Can anyone conceive of any other country whose citizens would respond to such a U.N. judgement by saying the criteria must be wrong? What is at work here is not modesty. It is the opposite. It is an assumption, a quite arrogant assumption, that what is successful in Canada is individual people, or particular parts of the country; an assumption that the whole community doesn't amount to much, doesn't contribute much. We need a little more modesty about ourselves, a little less about our extraordinary country.

Because we don't value our whole country enough, our attention has focused on our differences, our discontents, rather than upon the unique national community we have built together.

As in many societies, the loudest voices now are local — speaking of language, or province, or the interest of a particular group — and often they are frustrated or angry.

That phenomenon is part of modern life, from the most strident interest groups in the United States, to Welsh or Basque or Serb or Kurdish nationalists, to the opinion polls which have dragged down governments whose only common characteristic was that they were in office in an angry time.

The difference in Canada is that these localizing forces are pulling at a centre that has already become very weak. When I speak of the "centre," I am not talking, as a constitutionalist might, about the formal powers of the national government. I am speaking instead of the legitimacy of the Canadian idea, the idea of a large community, characterized by respect and compromise and common purpose.

That idea led to the development of a Canadian society that is admired around the world. Ironically, at home, in Canada, we have lost sight of our country as a whole community, and the more we see it just in parts, the more it comes apart.

For a long time, as a practical matter, French-speaking and English-speaking Canadians had little to do with one another. Through most of the 1950s, the country, including its Parliament and government, functioned mainly in English, and, in Quebec, an old regime encouraged French Canada to look inward and backward. There was not much occasion for the governments, let alone the people, of Alberta and Quebec ever to meet.

In addition, travel took more time then, so people travelled less. The media worked in print rather than the hotter and more immediate images of television. Economic decisions were concentrated much more exclusively in Toronto and Montreal, and, whatever frustration that might have caused elsewhere, there were no practical means to change that imbalance. National politics was dominated by one party. National prosperity meant there was no strong itch to change. Most of the country was white, and most of the immigration from Europe. Native people were denied the vote. Women were mainly in the kitchen, certainly not prominent in the professions or management or public life.

Nostalgia is powerful, and, to some, that period has taken on the aura of a golden age. That nostalgia is often the standard against which they judge contemporary Canada, and they believe many of our current problems are self-induced and, more to the point, artificial.

In 1991, just after I had taken the constitutional portfolio, one of my most loyal supporters had driven me to a meeting of local councillors in my constituency of Yellowhead. My friend supported me despite my views, because we disagreed on everything from bilingualism to capital punishment to immigration. I had asked the councillors what we might do to generate more pride in Canada, and reduce the general sense of antagonism that was boiling up then in Alberta. My friend entered the conversation and said: "You know, Joe, I used to be proud of Canada" – a long pause – "but it's changed."

He was speaking about 1950s Canada – which, in hindsight, he remembered as prosperous, predominantly English-speaking, relatively uncomplicated, and a society where most of the immigrants came, as he himself had, from Europe. Nostalgia is notoriously selective, and he had forgotten that was also a time, in Alberta, when Canadians of Ukrainian heritage had to Anglicize their names to get worthwhile jobs.

Since there is so little direct contact, it is easier for misunderstandings to take root, and grow. Nothing brought that home to me more forcibly than the reaction of my own father when he came with me to Chicoutimi on one of my visits as leader of the opposition.

My father had visited Quebec before, for conventions of the Canadian Weekly Newspapers Association and, indeed, had told me of the beauty and hospitality of Lac Saint-Jean, after he and other editors had travelled there by boat, up the Tadoussac.

Moreover, in animated debates at home in High River, he had defended his son's defence of the Official Languages Act. That's a little like supporting the Maple Leafs in the Forum, or wearing a turban to a Reform meeting, but he held his ground. It seemed to him to be fair that Quebecers should be able to speak French in their country.

The leader of the opposition doesn't travel alone in Chicoutimi. While civic officials are sometimes indifferent, party officials are anxious to be seen in the presence. There had been careful negotiation about who would ride with "the Leader," and one consequence was that my father and I travelled in separate cars. When we got together in our hotel room, he reported, with some astonishment: "They don't speak English here at all."

On his previous visits to Quebec, his hosts had provided translation, or made their point in whatever English they commanded. So his impression had been that, while French was the primary language, English was widely spoken in Quebec. To him, until that moment, official bilingualism had been an appropriate courtesy, to people who could speak English but found French easier. Until he found himself in a car with enthusiastic partisans with whom he couldn't speak, he had no reason to know that large parts of Quebec are as unilingually French as most of Alberta is unilingually English.

My father had assumed that Quebecers could speak English if they chose to. It had not occurred to him that there were large numbers of Quebec citizens who simply could not talk to their own government in English, couldn't discuss their tax returns, or some complex problem with their pension, unless, by luck, they found a French-speaking public servant.

And if that had not occurred to him, it was safe to assume there were thousands of other Albertans who believed that Quebecers could speak English if they chose to, and who, being less generous than my father, thought bilingualism was neither a courtesy, nor a requirement, but an imposition.

Those misunderstandings abound, and often only accidents reveal them. To celebrate Canada's 125th birthday, the Canada 125 program was devised to bring young people from one part of Canada to another. To help demonstrate the non-partisan nature of the program, my constituency of Yellowhead, in western Alberta, was twinned with Jean Chrétien's constituency of Beauséjour, in New Brunswick. One hundred and twenty-five Yellowhead students travelled to Beauséjour, and an equal number of New Brunswickers came out to see western Alberta and the Rocky Mountains.

Weeks after the exchange, I received a letter from the mother of one of the Yellowhead students. She had lived her life in Alberta and, until her daughter visited the Acadian communities of Beauséjour, had not realized that there was a large French-speaking population in Atlantic Canada, with a rich and old tradition. She had, she said, been an outspoken opponent of bilingual programs before, but that position had been based upon misunderstandings that her daughter's trip had taken away.

In part, the Canadian problem is related simply to distance which sets and keeps us physically apart, and intensifies the differences of geography and culture and climate, which make it hard for us to imagine parts of Canada where we have never been.

For example, for Torontonians who might contemplate a drive West, the prairie is not an invitation but a barrier – a long, dull, featureless expanse. For those of us who have lived there, the prairie is full of change and vistas and romance. I think, in fact, most Canadians who drive the Canadian prairie, particularly at night, become fascinated by the simple pull of the endless land. But, until you have tried it, the prospect of three straight days of Canadian Shield and prairie field is enough to divert the most ardent nationalist to Cape Cod.

I suspect a similar factor inhibits travel by English-speaking Canadians to Quebec. People are nervous about languages they don't speak, afraid that they will either miss important signals or be taken advantage of.

In 1979, because my party had won only two seats in Quebec, I scheduled a full Cabinet meeting in Quebec City, to demonstrate the new government's commitment to the whole of Canada. I wanted ministers' spouses to attend, because there were to be informal events designed to establish personal links. Many of the ministers, and most of their spouses, had never been to Quebec before, and fewer still had ever visited Quebec City. The barrier was not hostility, but difference. They had not felt comfortable enough to come.

That phenomenon exists in reverse; large numbers of Quebecers vacation only in Quebec and, often, when they vacation outside their province, establish French-speaking enclaves, in Maine or Florida, where *La Presse* is sold in the newsstands and French is spoken as much as English.

And in part, the Canadian problem is that our pragmatic, low-key country does not inspire the binding myths enshrined by more messianic societies and, indeed, is uncomfortable with public patriotism.

Even without those differences, the distances alone are daunting in Canada. Victoria, British Columbia, and St. John's, Newfoundland, are farther from each other than Tokyo is from

Chicago, and nearly twice as far as the distance between Nairobi, Kenya, and Paris, France. The flight from St. John's to Victoria is hours longer than that from St. John's to London, England.

In spring and summer, though temperatures in Canada are very attractive, many Canadians find it easier to go south than to stretch across the prairies, or travel to Atlantic Canada or Quebec.

So the points of reference they experience directly are in another country, and what they know of other communities in Canada comes secondhand. Increasingly, that secondhand information is freighted with false perceptions, and sometimes with prejudice.

Nothing proves that more dramatically than the controversy about cornflakes, and why the label on the box is in both French and English. The answer always seemed straightforward to me: the Kellogg's people wanted to sell their flakes to Canadians who eat breakfast in French and to Canadians who eat their breakfast in English. It was a simple marketing decision. If cornflakes had been advertised only in French in High River, a lot of the regulars would switch to Cream of Wheat, or granola, not because they prefer it, but because they could read the box. It wouldn't surprise me if Quebecers have the same little hang-up, and that people in general are more inclined to buy a product with a label they can read.

This cornflakes controversy should be trivial, except that it reflects a willingness to think the worst of your compatriots, and is one of those silly irritants which wears you down. If I were a francophone whose business took me a month each year to both Calgary and Denver, I am reasonably sure that, within that month, someone in Calgary would be on my back about the language of cornflakes. In Denver, it wouldn't cross anyone's mind to talk about cereal boxes.

To offset that kind of easy misunderstanding, we need to build upon experiences Canadians have in common. In 1991, a Citizens' Forum chaired by Keith Spicer travelled extensively across Canada, listening to complaints and looking for solutions. One of their recommendations was that exchange visits should be based upon an affinity or interest that already existed. For example, if there is to be an exchange of visits between Regina and Roberval, an effort should be made to have farmers visit farmers, and teachers visit teachers.

Certainly, my experience in a national political party demonstrated how quickly lasting bonds can be established among different Canadians. Successful Canadian parties are not primarily ideological; their purpose, on the contrary, is to provide a common base on which very different interests can come together. The members of Parliament elected, as Progressive Conservatives, in 1984 represented an extraordinary range of Canadian backgrounds, from people who had fought to keep the Union Jack as the flag of Canada to Quebec nationalists who had voted for sovereignty-association. With remarkably few exceptions, that caucus stayed together through nine controversial years, weathering deep internal differences on issues ranging from abortion to the Goods and Services Tax. A good part of the credit belongs to Prime Minister Mulroney's enormous skill in working with other people. But this was not an arranged harmony. It was as real as a family, and connected Canadians who, otherwise, might well have thought ill of one another. To take two prominent examples, Don Mazankowski and Benoît Bouchard come from opposite corners of Canada, and were further separated by different languages, styles, and interests. Yet they became close friends and allies, symbolizing the natural partnerships that will develop in Canada, if we give them a chance.

TWENTY-FIVE

CONSTITUTIONAL CHANGES

IT IS ONE THING TO HAVE SOME UNDERSTANDING OF THE PROBLEMS and opportunities in Canada, and quite another to have a clear sense as to what we might do about them. What follows does not come with a money-back guarantee, nor does it pretend to be a comprehensive solution to the problems facing Canada. However, it sets forth some practical actions that would let Canadians take control of our future, and not simply drift into a divorce we would all regret.

First, the bad news. We cannot save the country, or unite it, or rebuild it, without some formal constitutional change. So if you can't stand another word about the constitution, skip this chapter and go directly to the non-constitutional initiatives that follow. But I want there to be no doubt about my view. While it won't happen immediately, formal constitutional change is inevitable in Canada, and some of it will have to start fairly quickly. That is just another way of saying that there are some real things wrong in the way our country is organized today, and so there need to be some real changes in our rules and structures.

It is worth reflecting briefly on the constitutional developments of the last fifteen years, from the referendum in Quebec on "sovereignty-association," until today. The problem with the most recent constitutional debates, I think, is that they became disconnected from the everyday reality most Canadians were living. People were profoundly worried about their security and their jobs, and politicians were talking about "notwithstanding clauses" and a "third order of government." Add to that the corrosive cynicism which infected so much of public life, and it is not surprising that many Canadians regarded the constitutional talk as a cover for something else. In Quebec, the suspicion was that the process was a ruse to leave Quebec less than it needed; outside Quebec, it was the reverse: critics were convinced the constitutional discussions were a device to give Quebec more than it should have.

Those suspicions are still in the air, but we cannot let them shut down one of the instruments we need to renew the country. Perhaps an appropriate analogy is a car accident. Sometimes, people who have been in accidents will not ride in cars again. That means they do not go very far, just as we would not get very far, as a country, if we resolved to avoid constitutional change, and therefore leave our constitution in a form we know won't work. The better solution would be to drive more carefully next time.

With that in mind, let us look at some of the lessons to be drawn from our recent failures. Constitutional change is simply the form we give to political decisions to change the way we organize our community. While the focus is on the form of those changes, what is really important is their substance. Do we want to vest more control over education, and culture, and training, in governments that are closer to the citizens? Do we want to guarantee certain fundamental rights? Do we want the national government to set monetary policy, and foreign policy, and international trade policy? Do we want to recognize, in a formal way, the distinct society of Quebec? Do we want to recognize, formally, the inherent right to self-government within Canada of aboriginal peoples?

In the past, by and large, Canadian publics were prepared to accept the judgement of political leaders on those basic questions. Certainly – in the past – there was a widespread willingness to accept the judgement of leaders about what form those changes should take. Often there were great debates, between governments, or within Parliament and, frequently, political leaders did not get to the stage of seeking public support, because they themselves could not agree. That was the case with a series of proposed formulas to amend the constitution, and, for a long time, with policies respecting aboriginal people.

I think that deference to leaders began to change with the 1982 attempt to amend the constitution, and bring it home from Britain. My objectivity, on those events, may be suspect, because I was the Leader of Her Majesty's Loyal Opposition in Parliament at the time and, against the judgement of many in my party, had opposed that constitutional proposal the moment it was made. My caucus rallied behind me, and we forced the Trudeau government to allow televised parliamentary hearings on their proposals, where the questioning by MPs and senators, led by the Honourable Jake Epp, MP for Provencher, Manitoba, resulted in a widespread public interest. Naturally, our version of events is that our arguments and strategy were so effective that we stimulated that broad public interest.

In retrospect, I think there was also another factor. I believe that public response marked the beginning of a reaction against manipulation of constitutional issues by the national government. The Trudeau government had gone to great lengths to orchestrate support for their proposal. They had an elaborate game plan, set out in a document signed by now-Senator Michael Kirby and consequently known as the "Kirby Memorandum," which outlined a strategy to move the proposal past Parliament, the public, and the provinces, with as little debate as possible. This was 1981, a year after a similar orchestration by the Ottawa government had helped defeat sovereignty-association in the Quebec referendum, relying heavily on a promise by Mr. Trudeau that, if Quebec voted for Canada, there would be a "renewed federalism." Now, while there was no doubt that Ottawa was proposing a major change, it went in the opposite direction from what Quebecers thought they had been promised, as an incentive to vote for Canada.

So there was suspicion and anger in Quebec. Premiers in Western Canada were also sceptical or opposed. Their reasons ranged from the belief that a Charter of Rights was fundamentally inconsistent with Canadian tradition, to opposition to the proposed amending formula. But the proposal had been carefully crafted. It brought our constitution home to Canada from Britain, and who could oppose that? It proposed a formal Charter of Rights and Freedoms, and who could be against rights and freedoms? And it was an initiative, by a Canadian prime minister from Quebec, short months after the defeat of a separatist referendum question in that province.

Moreover, the Trudeau initiative was supported by the national leader of the New Democratic Party, and by the two Canadian premiers whose reputations seemed habitually to be the "most Canadian", and the least provincial, William Davis, of Ontario, and Richard Hatfield, of New Brunswick. To make life interesting for me, they were both Progressive Conservatives, members of my party, and they led governments, while I had just lost a national election. In the circumstances, it would not be surprising if the Trudeau government thought it could spin this past its critics relatively easily.

But that did not happen. Large numbers of Canadians became interested in the issues, and opposition spread. The Supreme Court ruled that the proposal, while acceptable in a strictly legal sense, did not respect adequately the constitutional conventions of Canada. When a modified proposal was finally accepted, divisions in the country had deepened, and the Canadian public was less willing to leave constitutional issues to their governments.

Certainly the fate of the Meech Lake and Charlottetown accords confirms that agreement by leaders is no longer enough on constitutional questions. From now on, before any significant constitutional change can take place, public consensus in support of the policy changes such amendments would reflect will have to be in place. That is why it is so critical now for Canadians to achieve a broader understanding of the real nature of our country. That is the only reliable basis upon which we can build the kind of consensus which will support significant constitutional change.

Ironically, constitutional reform, which will be essential to any real sense of unity and purpose in the country, has itself become an irritant. The constitutional impasse has exacerbated a sense of drift in the country. So, while we are building the consensus we need on constitutional change, we must rely on other means to generate broader understanding and a sense of national purpose. However, there should be no illusion, either that we can avoid constitutional change or that it will be easy.

Two basic dynamics have characterized recent controversies about the constitution. The first has been about who benefits. Traditionally, constitutional debate has focused on the nature and interests of Quebec. As an issue, "the constitution" had virtually become a synonym for "Quebec." Inside the province, and in some parts of the federal government, that created an almost proprietary sense that bridled when others asserted constitutional claims; elsewhere, naturally, that reaction generated both resentment and a suspicion that Quebec was not prepared to have the claims of other communities taken as seriously as its own.

The reality now is that other communities — aboriginals, women, the West — will be asserting a strong interest in a field where Quebec's claims have long been dominant. There is no necessary conflict between the interests of Quebec and the interests of these other Canadian communities, but the very novelty of a broader agenda creates its own tensions. For example, in my view, the Meech Lake Accord was not rejected because of what it contained, but rather because of whom it excluded. I am convinced that the reservations about the "distinct society" provisions of the accord would not have proven strong enough alone to bring it down. My view is that the basic motive was not an antipathy to Quebec, but a demand for fairness.

The other dynamic is more difficult, and goes back to the earliest discussions of the way the country should be structured. It is rooted in a tension between significant autonomy for provinces and "a strong central government." That was a constant theme in the discussions leading to the Charlottetown Accord, and the most creative attempt to bridge it was by the proposal to have "asymmetrical federalism" – a forbidding phrase that means treating different provinces differently. The concept would, for example, have given Quebec constitutional powers over culture that other provinces would not have, because questions of language and culture are more important to Quebec than to other provinces. As I have argued earlier, that concept is well established in Canadian history, and indeed is reflected in the constitution today. The political problem is that this approach amounts to "special status" and, in the present atmosphere, that is not a popular concept. It may be that, after calm and extended discussion, a consensus could be built in support of treating different provinces differently. That is certainly a result worth pursuing, because we are going to need some bridges to overcome the conventional differences about constitutional powers.

The issue is twofold. There is a substantive disagreement about what power is required at the centre of a large country in the modern world. Quebec, and now provinces like Alberta and British Columbia, believe they should have more power to develop their particular potential. Smaller and less wealthy provinces will continue to be extremely reluctant to accept any changes which might reduce the support they can expect from the country as a whole. On a less pragmatic, more philosophical, level, there is a fear that any decentralization would weaken the country's capacity to maintain, or advance, traditional Canadian social programs and political standards. The difference is not minor. On each side, it is almost an article of faith.

But beyond the substance, there is also a widespread assumption in Quebec that the rest of Canada would not be prepared to contemplate any real reduction in the power of the central government. They have heard arguments that Canada is the most decentralized federation in the world, and naturally conclude that Canadians who make that argument would have the central government hold what power it has. That raises a basic question about the credibility of the commitment, outside Quebec, to fundamental constitutional reform.

That question must be answered, because it speaks directly to the alliances Quebec might find in pursuing significant changes in the constitution, once negotiations began, if those negotiations were on the basis of rebuilding and renewing a united Canada. There is no doubt in my mind that, in those circumstances, the large majority of Canadians would accept changes which granted more constitutional powers to provinces. Some of those Canadians would not be enthusiastic, but would acquiesce in changes that would keep the country intact. In other cases, however, there is already a considered view that the national community would be stronger if its constituent parts had more power to develop their own potential.

Quebecers should not assume that they are the only Canadians who believe in a more flexible, less centralized, federation. In fact, they could only believe that if they had been paying no real attention to the discussion of constitutional issues over the last three decades in my own national party, or by the governments of influential provinces like Alberta and British Columbia. The actual record of constitutional discussion shows that both those provinces formally proposed arrangements that could have come from Quebec. Indeed, during most of the constitutional debates when René Lévesque and Peter Lougheed were the premiers, respectively, of Quebec and Alberta, they formed an effective and reliable alliance. A similar approach was the basis of the constitutional proposals placed on the table by Prime Minister Mulroney's government, and that general approach was accepted, unanimously, by all the provinces and territories in the Charlottetown Accord. Some Quebecers may argue that the movement on powers did not go far enough, but there can be no denial of the willingness of other governments, other legislatures, Parliament, and a large portion of the Canadian public, to move beyond the status quo. Just as significant was the readiness, during the discussions before the Charlottetown negotiation, of groups who traditionally support a "strong central government" to consider the concept of special status. That is further proof that there is substantial room to move on constitutional powers and jurisdiction.

It is true that, at one extreme of constitutional opinion outside Quebec, there is the view that the central government must keep, or even expand, its present powers, and that pressures for any increase in the jurisdiction or capacity of provinces must simply be faced down. That view leaves little room for negotiation and, in my view, could not be sustained in any serious discussion. It is simply not consistent with a genuine commitment to "renewed federalism."

Speaking personally, I have never worried much about whether we were more decentralized than other federations. Even were it true, what does it mean? Federalism is neither a beauty contest, nor a formula: there is not some fixed set of outside standards to which Canada must conform. It is instead the name we have given to flexible arrangements that let complex nations be who they are. We have to develop a system that works for Canada, a special country, whose needs and values and priorities are particular to us.

Ironically, other pressures may help us design new arrangements that will work. The truism is that the world is changing, and old assumptions need to be examined. That applies to

Canada as much as anywhere else, and, in our case, the reassess-
ment has been made more urgent by fiscal realities, and by the
growing proof that some of our most established systems aren't
achieving the goals we expect of them. For example, both those
factors influence the current debate over Canadian social policy.
Our accumulated debt means we cannot afford all of our present
programs, in their present form, particularly if we want to take
new social initiatives. At the same time, there is evidence of
some abuse and, more important, a clear indication that some
of our programs do not encourage the initiative and self-respect
which are part of their purpose. We are examining those social
programs on the basis of their results, and their cost, and that
will have little to do with theories of federalism or relative
degrees of centralization. Some of the most innovative reforms
being considered now involve governments working together,
as in the Canada-New Brunswick experiment in work experience and training called NB Works. It may be that the best way
to take account of new realities, and still respect traditional
Canadian values, will involve some changes in jurisdiction.

Critics of constitution-making distinguish between "real"
issues and constitutions. Let me adopt their typology to make
the point that, from now on, "real" and constitutional impera-
tives may work together. Social policy is not the only field where,
on the basis of results and cost and competition, we have to
review at a fundamental level the way we have been operating
in Canada. If we agree on new policy goals, it might be easier
to work out new constitutional arrangements.

In any event, we need a different, calmer, climate to achieve
significant constitutional change. We have been trying to fashion
concrete details of complex legal arrangements in almost impossible circumstances. On the last two occasions – the negotiations

at Meech Lake and Charlottetown — the presence of deadlines created a sense that people were being rushed to judgement, and that not enough care or time was being taken. More generally, the atmosphere of constitutional discussions has been highly charged by suspicion and misunderstanding.

Constitutional discussion became highly personalized after the election of Pierre Trudeau as Prime Minister of Canada in 1968, and René Lévesque as Premier of Quebec in 1976. The two came with a history of disagreement that was so strong that other attitudes became marginalized, and other realities virtually irrelevant.

I speak from some experience. If you believed the world was divided into two camps, I was assumed to be in the Trudeau camp, because I was a federalist and a member of Parliament. Yet I thought his view of my country was fundamentally wrong, and my disagreements with him on constitutional questions were far more serious than on other issues. That became understood by a small group of Quebec journalists and intellectuals, who had no perceptible impact on public opinion in Quebec, and then it became crystal clear in the fight over Mr. Trudeau's charter and patriation package, in 1981. But, in the late 1970s, no one much noticed, certainly not voters in Quebec. (That reality was driven home to me on May 24, 1977, when there were five federal by-elections in Quebec. We had attracted good candidates and, to our surprise, had won some editorial endorsements from the Quebec media. We were clobbered in each by-election.)

That dramatic contest between Pierre Trudeau and René Lévesque concealed a wealth of more moderate attitudes in the country as a whole. Robert Stanfield had deliberately and profoundly changed the attitude of his national party on Canadian unity questions. The words "Stanfield" and "revolution" do not fit easily in the same sentence, yet he took a party which had just torn itself apart opposing the Maple Leaf flag for Canada; directed it through an Official Languages Act whose purpose, in part, was to divide the Progressive Conservative party; and transformed it into a party which Quebecers and other Canadians were prepared to trust. That is a story for another time, but it demonstrates dramatically, in actions not words, that English-Canadian leaders, and the larger public of Canada, can come to positions which reasonable Quebecers can find comfortable.

But the suspicion is profound. In 1979, there was a vacancy in the Supreme Court of Canada that was to be filled by a lawyer from Quebec. The prime minister names judges to the Supreme Court and, after consultation with Jacques Flynn, my minister of Justice, and others, I decided on a list of three nominees, from which I would choose one. Then I phoned the premier of Quebec, Mr. Lévesque, told him I was planning to nominate one person from that list, and asked if he or his ministers had any considered objection to any of the candidates.

It was one of my first dealings with Mr. Lévesque, and he was instantly suspicious. "Why are you calling me?" he asked. I told him that the constitutional convention was that this vacancy should be filled by a Quebecer and, while the authority was clearly mine, I knew the great sensitivity of Quebec governments to the Supreme Court. "No one has ever done this before," Lévesque replied. I said that I couldn't speak for the past but, as prime minister now, I would welcome a reply, on an entirely confidential basis, as to whether the Government of Quebec judged any of the nominees to be unacceptable. Premier Lévesque thanked me, said he would call the next day, and, at precisely 9:00 a.m., telephoned to advise that Quebec had no objection to any of the names, and to thank me for the courtesy. Days later, the Honourable Julien Chouinard was named to the Supreme Court, where he served with distinction until his tragic and premature death.

Mr. Lévesque had seen me in the image of my predecessor, Mr. Trudeau. Undoubtedly, many Quebecers see the rest of Canada in the image of hard-line constitutional positions that have been taken in the past, or extreme actions offensive to Quebec, such as the widely televised wiping of rural Ontario feet on the Quebec flag. That is not an accurate picture of Canada – not accurate respecting general attitudes, nor about the approach to the constitution. But it is widespread, and it is one source from which the new support for separatism flows.

The real issue is not which government has jurisdiction over training, or culture, or tourism, or any other specific field. The issue is whether Canada is serious about the most compelling promise made by the federalist side during the 1980 referendum – the undertaking that, if Quebec voted for Canada, there would be a fundamental renewal of the Canadian federation. There is no question that that promise was made, and there can be little doubt that it had an influence, probably a decisive influence, on the referendum result. Most Quebecers believe, as do I, that that promise has not been kept. In that sense, the best way to deal with future referenda in Quebec is to keep the promise Canada made in the first referendum.

The question now is how do we provide Quebecers with a reasonable assurance that, when the time comes to go back to a negotiating table, there would be significant constitutional change. The immediate need is not for detailed proposals, cobbled together on another road to Damascus, but rather for a reliable signal that serious Canadians, outside Quebec, understand that the survival of a large Canada requires a significant reform of our federation, and are committed to working for that kind of reform. Even that would be treated with scepticism by many Quebecers, who would argue that the time is past for promises and signals. But scepticism is not fatal. If the signal were serious, it would have an effect.

What would that signal require, to be taken seriously? What I have in mind is a project which would ask a group of credible Canadians to design a federation for the twenty-first century in Canada. This would not be simply an amendment of the status quo. Instead, they should start by identifying the purposes Canadians want their constitution to achieve, and then develop and examine specific options that would work in the modern country Canada is becoming. I am not proposing that we throw out the present constitution. It was developed deliberately and for good reason, and its merits would recommend themselves. But the project should not be confined by what we have now. It needs to reach well beyond our present arrangements, and should therefore be seen as a political process, identifying goals and the way to reach them, rather than as a legal exercise.

It seems to me that at least four elements would be necessary.

First, while the group should not be bound to the status quo, neither should it be theoretical. The project would have to attract the participation of Canadians who have experience with the issues, and are not hostile to the idea of significant reform. Those should include people with practical experience in how governments and constitutions work – former premiers, former federal and provincial parliamentarians, aboriginal leaders, and a small group of constitutional experts. It would also need to attract other citizens who do not claim to be formal experts, but are knowledgeable, and have thought practically about what would be needed to make a federation that would enable contemporary Canadians to work together effectively. Some method of voluntary selection, similar to the process by which so-called ordinary Canadians were involved in 1982 would make sense.

Second, this would not be formal constitutional negotiation, nor would it have any official status that would limit the reach of the project. There would not be delegates. It would operate at arm's length from government, but with a realistic sense of what governments might accept, and what would likely prove impossible.

Third, there should be a clear understanding that the project is designed explicitly to identify an arrangement which would encourage citizens of Quebec to choose to stay Canadian. That purpose cannot slide off the table, or the whole venture would fail. However, the question is Canada, so the purpose is to design a federation that works for the whole country. As a practical matter, equal priority must be given to aboriginal, institutional, and other issues.

Finally, this project should proceed in tandem with urgent campaigns to improve the understanding Canadians have of one another, and of our sense of worth and purpose as a national community. In time, the constitutional project would have to yield concrete proposals, some of which would have to depart sharply from familiar arrangements. That would work only in the context of a serious campaign to improve understanding among Canadians, so there would be a political consensus from which those changes might flow.

Everything I know about Canada leads me to believe that such a consensus exists in the country, and only needs to be brought out. But there is no point in achieving agreement on the nature and purpose of the country without having some practical proposals about new arrangements which could express that consensus. We need a thorough-going initiative to examine the options that would be the basis of those practical new arrangements.

One of the lessons you learn in Parliament is that every word you utter there is recorded in Hansard, the official record of the debates of the House of Commons, and your opponents will often bring back those words to taunt you. As I make this suggestion, I am well aware that, shortly after I was appointed the minister responsible for Constitutional Affairs, I resisted a proposal made by many Canadians that we should step outside Parliament and establish a "constituent assembly" to bring forth a new constitutional proposal. I raised two objections then. The first was that we were embarked, in 1991, on a formal constitutional process that had to yield some agreement among governments before a Quebec referendum in twelve to eighteen months. Among other things, that process had to deal directly with the specific issues that had been rejected in the failure of the Meech Lake Accord. I was not confident that a wholly new approach would let us meet deadlines and requirements which would be criticial to any success.

My other objection was to the view that parliamentarians had lost their legitimacy, and therefore their most important roles should be assumed by some new "representatives" who would emerge from an extraordinary process. I thought, and think, that such a turning away from Parliament would weaken, seriously and permanently, the authority of that institution to deal with crisis. But I also doubted whether the credibility of some new arrangement would survive public cynicism very long. I was convinced that the contagion which discredited people elected to the established institution of Parliament would quickly immobilize new representatives produced by a process which had no tradition or roots.

Whether I was right or wrong then, the present situation is different in three respects. First, there is no formal constitutional process or agenda, and probably there should not be one, given the fatigue with traditional constitutional issues and the volatility of the separatist campaign in Quebec. So this project would not compete with the work of governments. Second, there is no parliamentary process, and therefore no reflection on the capacity or authority of the body elected to decide critical issues for Canadians. And finally, while this project would have its greatest value in proposing options which can be adopted, its immediate purpose is to demonstrate that Canadians across the country share with Quebecers a determination to keep the promise of the 1980 referendum, and achieve a fundamental renewal of the Canadian federation. A project of that kind is one important element of the actions we should be taking, right now, to keep and build our country.

TWENTY-SIX

WHAT INDIVIDUAL
CITIZENS CAN DO

PUBLIC FIGURES CAN'T ESCAPE CARTOONISTS. CERTAINLY, I NEVER could. It turns out that I was treated more generously at the end of my public life than at the beginning. To the cartoonists, my career went from "Joe Who" when I burst upon an unsuspecting nation in my party's 1976 convention, to "Captain Canada" during the constitutional debate. Renown, these days, is solemnized in sweatshirts, and students at the Grande Cache High School, in my constituency, gave me one with those words emblazoned on the back. (To keep things in perspective, a few months later, the people of Grande Cache joined most other Canadians in voting against Captain Canada's proposals.)

Among the implications of that title was the idea that, at some point of maximum peril, I would duck into a phone booth, or shout "Shazam!" and summon superhuman powers to solve

Canada's problems. Then the country could go back to serious issues, like the deficit, or the Blue Jays. Like most cartoons, the Captain Canada caricature reflected some genuine public attitudes, including the sense that resolving Canada's differences would require heroic intervention that was beyond the power of ordinary citizens.

I believe the opposite. The only way we can unite and renew this country is through the active, caring commitment of individual Canadians. Obviously, we also need ingenuity, and vision, and generosity, from Canadians who are looked to as leaders. And we will need to change some of our practices and arrangements, including, inevitably, parts of our constitution. But we are not talking about a legal or economic proposition, where experts prevail; we are talking about a country, a place where people live and dream and frame their futures, a national community that is losing its hold on its citizens. The simple truth is that, at this point in the life of Canada, our country can work only if its people want it to.

I don't say that as either a romantic or an outsider. My whole life has been in "the system"; my reputation is as a pragmatist. I have had the opportunity to come to know our institutions more thoroughly than most Canadians and, as a consequence, probably respect them more, and I have ample reason to admire the experts who make their extraordinary talents available to Canada. We will need them all. But we have to recognize that there has been a basic change in the nature of the challenge to Canada. The pressures are no longer limited to the nationalism of Quebec, and the solutions will have to go beyond constitutional adjustments.

In effect, Canada, as a large modern federation, is facing the kinds of challenges that have shaken giant corporations. The problem is not confined to one aspect of our lives, but rather reaches to our structures and purpose. This is not a little local difficulty that will yield to conventional prescriptions. And because we are a country, and not a corporation, bound together by much more complex goals than profit, the only way we can succeed is with broad public support. I am not so naïve as to believe that public enthusiasm about Canada will magically translate into the practical solution of all our problems. My argument, instead, is that, without public enthusiasm about Canada, no amount of ingenuity or creative delay will reverse the drift that is gradually pulling our country apart. And soon we could reach a point where we have drifted too far, and the parts cannot be pulled together again.

I believe there are some practical initiatives which can, and should, be pursued by Canadians to whom others look for leadership. But the rock upon which we will renew our country, or see it founder, is the will of Canadian citizens themselves. I am convinced there is a will, across the country, to choose and sustain a large and modern community, but it must become more assertive.

From my perspective, the most encouraging single aspect of the Charlottetown process was the degree to which individual citizens came to the aid of their country. It has become popular to disparage élites, and, after the referendum, some perverse satisfaction was taken from the fact that the counsel of so many leaders, local and national, was rejected when Canadians voted "No." Yet there is nothing unusual, in these times, about élites being rejected. What is more striking, in the Canadian context, is how many people who were not normally involved in "national" debates became involved in that campaign — from mayors of municipalities, large and small, to farm leaders, to the

Canadian Legion, to local Chambers of Commerce and the B.C. Federation of Labour, to homemakers chairing "Yes" committees. These are people who made a connection between the well-being of their local community and the integrity of their country, and then put their personal reputations on the line, often in hostile circumstances. That has not happened before, in anything like that degree, and is both a proof of a strong commitment to Canada and a resource to mobilize again.

I am very much aware that many people who supported the "Yes" campaign in the referendum had serious reservations about particular parts of the accord, and their motive was to affirm their country, not every detail of that agreement. By the same token, most of those who voted "No" were voting against some provision of the accord, or against its proponents, rather than against the country.

There are important differences between 1992 and now. For most of Canada, there is no specific question to consider, no referendum to approve or disapprove. There are no structures, no formal incentives, which might cause Canadians to talk about their country, to reach beyond their region. Outside Quebec, there is a sense of being spectators at the debate about our future, rather than participants. In those circumstances, two practical questions arise about Canadians' will to make our country work. The first is how to express that will where it exists, and the second is how to encourage it where it does not.

Every voyage may start with a single step, but that first step is a whopper, particularly when you are one citizen, out of 27 million, trying to influence the attitudes of people you don't know, on issues you don't fully understand. Yet the challenge is to take an initiative, not be an expert, and most of us have had to step into something new before.

When I first sought my party's nomination in the spectacular constituency of Rocky Mountain — which contained the three national parks of Jasper, Banff, and that small gem tucked in the southwest corner of Alberta, Waterton Lakes — there were literally hundreds of communities where I knew no one. The riding sprawled from the Peace River country, down the Rockies, to the U.S. border, and the people I knew were concentrated west of the fifth meridian, out of High River. I was running against a very able Liberal member of Parliament, Allan Sulatacky, and there was only a handful of card-carrying federal Progressive Conservatives. So, I had to build a lot of the organization myself, relying upon people I could recruit. Naturally, I sought help from supporters of my provincial party and I knocked on a lot of doors, calling cold. But I also drew up a list of the names of the towns and villages in Rocky Mountain, and sent that list to friends elsewhere in Alberta, asking them who they knew in Lodgepole, or Sangudo, or Cynthia, or Seebe, or Peers, or Hillcrest, or the other places I wanted to represent in Parliament. That yielded a list of at least one hundred names, people to whom I suddenly had a personal connection, and, after I went to visit, a large number of those people worked or voted for me.

Most of you who have been active in your local community would have a similar story. There was something you thought should be done, so you built a network, and got it done. Across this country, there are swimming pools, and wilderness trails, and scholarships, and drop-in centres, and uniforms for the church choir or the school team that trace their origin back to a citizen or a group who took an initiative. That do-it-yourself ethic runs deep in Canada, and what has worked locally can also work in this very personal country. Let me suggest some ways.

A. At Home

1. Start some discussions about Canada. Either draw together some neighbours or go through a local service club, or church group, or other organization. Focus on a particular topic – for example, Quebec nationalism, or aboriginal self-government, or Senate reform. Find some background material that can be circulated and serve as the basis of discussion; at the risk of sounding self-serving, the chapters in this book on the West, the aboriginal community, or Quebec would be one place to start. Invite a teacher or a community leader or any wise person to serve as moderator. Organize the early discussion, so the issues can be raised in an orderly way, and then encourage questions and debate. If the discussion works, organize others, widening your reach.

2. Invite speakers, either to informal neighbourhood discussions or to meetings of existing organizations. It will not be hard to find interesting speakers about Canada. Local schools or colleges will have faculty members who have studied specialized fields, whether early Norse settlements in Newfoundland, or the history of your own community or region. Almost certainly, there are, among your neighbours, people who come from other parts of Canada, and are proud of where they came from, and would welcome talking about it. In your business community, or trade unions, or churches, you would find citizens who have direct and objective experience of other parts of Canada, or who have seen, firsthand, conditions in other countries and the international standing which Canada enjoys. Neighbours who immigrated here, from other countries, may be prepared to talk about what drew them to Canada, what surprised them when they

came, what they think now. National aboriginal organizations would either send speakers themselves, or recommend people close at hand who could tell their story. So would other national organizations – the banks, the RCMP, women's organizations, and various public policy groups. The point would be to use speakers to generate more understanding of the Canada you don't yet know, and then expand that process, to draw new people in.

3. Use your local library, not just for heavy reference books about Canada, but for books or stories from other parts of our country. It might be very useful to draw some friends together simply to look at some of the magnificent books of pictures of Canada, which often convey a sense of both the land and its people. Again, see if the library can give you two weeks' worth of newspapers from some other province, so you can see if the news is treated differently, and whether and how the editorial commentary changes. Get in touch with the National Film Board, and draw on their powerful library of films about Canada. Their address in Ottawa is Mercury Court, 179 Rideau Street, Ottawa, ON, K1A 0M9, and they have local offices across the country. If your travels have taken you to some town whose atmosphere you liked, subscribe to their community newspaper, to keep in touch with the events and perspectives which create that atmosphere.

4. Speak up for your country. Remind your friends, and family, about the U.N. judgement that Canada is the best place in the world to live. When the television news reports riots elsewhere in the world, and prejudice, and people who can't get medical care, remember the community we have built here. Fly your Canadian flag, not just on July 1, but every day. Display a Canadian map, or landscape, in your home or where you work.

5. Be prepared to defend the country. Too many Canadians speak badly of Canada, almost in passing. Often, they may not mean what they say but, if no other voice is raised, their negative view is what registers. I'm not recommending fierce debates or fisticuffs. But if somebody casually maligns the Native peoples, or Quebec, or some other Canadian, you might ask them why they hold that view, or whether they have ever met a Native Canadian, or been to Quebec.

B. Reaching Out.

1. Call your friends in other parts of the country – the people you do business with, or knew at school, or went to church with before they moved – and talk with them about Canada. If you think there is a danger of the country drifting apart, say why, and indicate what you are thinking of doing about it. Ask what they think. Ask them how the people in their province view your province. Encourage them to get active in their community, and to compare notes and ideas.

2. If you are travelling to some other part of Canada, build in a few extra days, or hours, and go somewhere you haven't been before. Get out of the city centres, into neighbourhoods or towns. If there is a local game or a concert, go to it. Visit the museum or any local historic site. Talk to people in restaurants or stores. Ask them about their community, and tell them about yours. So much travel today takes place in a vacuum. We take familiar routes, meet the usual people, and spend our free time phoning home. People who are often in Montreal or Toronto or Calgary have never been to the Beauce or the Danforth or the Badlands, where the atmosphere is different.

3. Plan a visit to some part of Canada you haven't seen before. Read about it first, so you'll have some sense of what to look for. Take materials from home that describe the culture or economy or advantages of your own community, so you can open a dialogue. Make a point of talking to people, and seeing things you wouldn't find at home. Don't worry about language, whether French or English or the other languages which predominate in other Canadian communities, and don't hesitate to raise questions which trouble you. Don't look on it as a duty. Tourists from around the world are fascinated by Canada, and you would be too.

4. Check with convention organizers, or tourist officials, to see who is coming to visit. Conventions, or sporting events, draw delegates or spectators from across the country. Some of them see nothing more of your community than a hotel room or a stadium. They might welcome a chance to see more, and would find it hard to remain indifferent to a place which extended that hand.

C. FORMAL ORGANIZATIONS

1. Networks of service clubs connect communities, large and small, across Canada. They focus on local service, but each has been involved in national campaigns, ranging from the Rotary Adventure in Citizenship which first brought me to Ottawa, to the vigorous role of the Kinsmen and Kinettes in encouraging Canadians to fly our flag. Most of those organizations have French-speaking clubs in Quebec and English-speaking ones elsewhere, and are active in the various cultural communities in Canada. They have already established a common base across the country, and are ideally placed to draw their members more

closely together. They should encourage joint projects, reaching from region to region, more exchanges, or holidays in one another's communities.

2. Fiscal realities may not allow extensive government-funded youth exchange programs. But there should be an exploration of the capacity of private organizations to undertake more focused exchanges. For example, in 1992, I had discussed a self-funded exchange between Unifarm, the Alberta farmers' organization, and the Toronto Chinese Benevolent Association, which would bring young urban Chinese Canadians to visit rural Alberta, and youngsters from Alberta farm families to Toronto (in baseball season). That particular initiative fell through when I left the Cabinet, but the model is worth pursuing.

3. More national enterprises are incorporating Canadian symbols and themes in their advertising and product promotion. That practice should be encouraged, and joint initiatives considered. In 1992, the MP Dennis Mills, the Toronto Maple Leafs, and others organized a national midget hockey tournament that brought teams and young players from all provinces together in the Gardens, and that is another venture to emulate.

4. Each year, national organizations hold annual meetings or conventions which draw their members together from across Canada. Each group has its own agenda, but there is a common interest in Canada, and that should be asserted much more deliberately. The best means may be to provide specific occasions for small groups from different parts of Canada to sit down together to discuss their goals for their country.

TWENTY-SEVEN

A SENSE OF
PURPOSE

THERE IS NO "QUICK FIX" FOR A COUNTRY. WHETHER YOUR GOAL is to hold together the existing Canada or to launch a separate Quebec, or to build the country we know into a more purposeful and compelling community, it will take time, and skill, and ingenuity, to achieve. That is particularly true today, because the forces that break down societies are strong and pervasive. Ironically, that is a factor which would have to be considered by a sovereign Quebec as surely as it would by the larger Canada. The territory which separatists mean by "Quebec" includes very diverse populations, ranging from aboriginal people to anglophones and francophones whose roots reach back generations; to significant populations originally from Asia, Africa, Haiti, the Middle East, and much of Europe, some of them deeply rooted in Quebec, some very recently arrived. The lessons of the collapsed Soviet Union, and Eastern and Central Europe after the

Berlin Wall, indicate that the easiest time for new nations is the moment of independence itself, and then the euphoria gives way to hard economic, ethnic, and political realities. Obviously, Quebec is not an impoverished republic, just as Canada is not the old Soviet Union. The point is that the modern world tests the mettle of every national community, large or small, new or established.

In one sense, the very threat of separation means Canadians are more vulnerable to those pressures than are comparable countries where there is no such threat. We cannot count on a status quo; it is simply not a realistic option, in a country facing all the contemporary Canadian pressures for change. If we break up, all our parts would be more exposed to international pressures and internal tensions. If we simply patch together the existing federation, the world will know, and we will know, that there must be more changes later, maybe deep changes. If we are to keep the country together but transform the way it works and sees itself, that, by definition, involves change and risk.

National sovereignty doesn't mean what it used to. That is true in terms of law, simply because every nation must surrender some of its control over itself to gain more influence over others. If we want Europe to take down its trade barriers to our goods, we must take down our barriers to Europe's goods. If we want the international agency that tests nuclear plants to have authority in North Korea, we have to give it the same authority in Canada. If we want an acid-rain treaty with the United States, we have to agree to have the same kinds of controls on emissions in Canada that they do in the United States. Those international rules are designed to make the world more secure, and more certain, but they impose real limits upon the independence of each country.

Of course, that fact reaches well beyond laws and treaties. The international economy works on a world-wide basis. It respects the laws of nations, but judges their policies impersonally, and often harshly. Individual countries – an independent Canada, an independent Quebec – decide the content of their national policies, but the world economy decides the consequences of those policies. That is not a conspiracy, but simply the way the modern world works. It is less true of superpowers than of fledgling states, less true of large countries than of small ones, but no one is immune, and that makes a profound difference in the practical meaning of national independence.

Beyond the economy, fashion and music and ideas reach automatically across borders. CNN is the symbol of the way media images leap around the world, affecting opinion at the same instant in Calgary and Calcutta, Montreal and Johannesburg. That impact was driven home to me during the Gulf War. Moments after the prime minister announced Canada's decision to send Canadian fighter planes to the Gulf, I informed our allies, including U.S. Secretary of State Jim Baker, whose plane had just landed in Cairo. He came on the phone to say: "I just saw on CNN that you are sending planes to the Gulf." That same power of media to reach over borders was clear years before the Berlin Wall came down. Communist officials in the East tried to jam broadcasts from the West, and every expensive blocking device they invented was broken, almost instantly, by some new technique or act of ingenuity. For better or worse, no place is isolated any more.

As a practical matter, that wide-open world offers special challenges to Western democracies because our citizens have both the economic luxury and the political freedom to consider and embrace new fashions and ideas. It is harder for our societies to enforce a common line, including a common sense of purpose or patriotism. That is true even in countries where patriotism is second nature, as the reaction in the United States to the Vietnam War proved. So it constitutes a real challenge in a more diffident country like Canada, where many of the traditional instruments of unity have lost legitimacy.

That is to say we cannot bring and keep Canada together by artificial means. The only arguments that will work are true arguments; any sense of purpose must be real. That seems to me to be a reasonable proposition. We should not try to keep together a country that would be better off apart. By the same token, we should not force apart a country which, on its merits, should be together.

The challenge is to judge those merits. Some of them are intangible and emotional – the friendships, history, and associations that have grown over seven decades; the reputation of Canada. Others are very tangible, and practical – the practices and contracts, the pensions and protections, the agreements and joint ventures, the shared obligations of Canadians. But the assessment that would be most interesting, and most valuable, would be that which judged how our interests would best be served in the future, in the world we see emerging. We should look at that with the clearest of eyes, and not be diverted by threats, or mythology, or short temper.

It may be that we talk too much about the past. It is important, because it framed us, made us what we are. But we have found, in the last thirty years of this self-conscious debate, that we are more aware of the histories that set us apart than we are of the history we have lived together. For some reason, Albertans remember the National Energy Program, and Quebecers remember the rejection of Meech Lake, more acutely than either remembers medicare or sustained economic growth or the consistent commendation of the world community. Probably, with effort, we can change that, and a simple respect for perspective should make us try. But that won't happen quickly.

In any event, the past is not where we are going to live and grow. Our world has been transformed by changes which most of our parents would have dismissed as science fiction, and the world of our children will be even more different. That is the world we should be preparing for. I grew up in a time when the sixty-kilometre drive to Calgary was a long journey and a big event. When my father had been a boy, that trip took two days, and he used to show me the "half-way house" where travellers would stay overnight. In my daughter's generation, people walk on the moon, human life is conceived in laboratories, and the market for what we produce is not down the road but across the globe. In that contemporary world, the real tests to our society will not come from language laws, or geographic tensions, or the other old issues we debate in the name of the constitution, but from these new realities.

It would be extremely helpful to all of us to find a fresh way to look at our future. There needs to be a clear focus on the goals of modern Canada – the tests we are going to face together, the purposes which a modern community should seek to achieve, whatever political boundaries it establishes. It is time to define ourselves by what we want to do, and what we need to do, in the future, rather than what we might have failed to do in the past.

A good approach would be to focus on modern issues we are all going to have to face, whatever flag we fly. That very process would give us a good idea as to whether we are more likely to resolve those issues alone or together. It would let the future define Canada, rather than just the past.

One model would be to have independent institutes of public policy organize a small series of national meetings on Canadian goals, along the general lines of the six constitutional conferences. Obviously, that model could be improved, to take account of weaknesses that emerged in the first incarnation. But that model has real advantages, including a track record of some success, in circumstances roughly comparable to the doubts and divisions we face today. The sponsorship would have to be respectable and independent, and could involve some or all of the institutes which carried the 1992 meetings. There should be substantial participation by so-called ordinary Canadians, who would nominate themselves, and be chosen by an impartial jury. Organizations with a clear interest in the specific topic could be invited to partipate, on the condition that they not come in an adversarial frame of mind. There could be venues across the country, with all proceedings open to the media, and a genuine discussion, designed to lead to some consensus.

These would be national conferences on goals, not means; purposes, not processes. Topics could include issues which any national government, under any flag, would have to consider in modern North America. They could be generic: how to compete and maintain prosperity; how to respect diverse communities within a modern nation-state; how to contribute constructively to international peace and security; what values should guide a community in a world where science has lifted so many traditional constraints; what are the practical expressions of sovereignty and identity in the modern world. Or they could be more specific, focusing on competitiveness with Asia or the European Union, or the interface with the United States, or relations with aboriginal peoples. But their principal purpose would be to look forward to the real issues which any government, and any people, in northern North America will have to face. In the process, I expect we would discover whether we share enough real goals and real interests to justify working together in one country.

My expectation is that we would find ample cause to stay together as one large community. But the reason for proposing a focus on goals is not simply that I think it would reveal common ground. It is also a far more sensible basis for a country to decide its future than a debate on the constitution or grievances. And it holds the prospect of yielding a sense of purpose, which could then become the basis of renewing Canada, with an eye on the future, rather than the past.

TWENTY-EIGHT

This Is Canada's Time

IT IS SAID THAT GENERALS ALWAYS PREPARE FOR THE LAST WAR, because that is what they know. That truth applies to more than generals, and certainly it describes the so-called unity debate in Canada, where the most passionate discussion has been about our past, rather than our future. In fact, it has been about a past which we remember badly, and interpret differently; so, in that sense, it has not been a debate at all, but rather an exchange of misunderstandings, grievances, and regrets. That is a foolish basis on which to end a successful country, or try to launch a new one. It would also mark a sharp departure from the pragmatism which has been part of our character for as long as life has been recorded here. We should be as pragmatic about changing our country as earlier Canadians were about building it. As we contemplate decisions which, one way or another, will profoundly affect the community in which our children live, and their children, let us think carefully about three elements of the life of this country: how we came to be; what we are today; what we might become.

In the beginning, there were only aboriginal people here, in small numbers, scattered across a vast continent. Then, other people came, from everywhere, some by careful choice, some for refuge, most because the opportunities seemed better here than where they were.

There is no single story to describe the motives of the people who actually pulled up roots. It is hard for me to imagine what courage or frustration it must have taken to leave behind friends and surroundings you could never regain, and go off into an unknown. Yet that is how the great majority of us got here. In each Canadian family, except those that are Indian or Inuit, someone took the deliberate decision to leave what they knew and come to Canada.

Some came as groups – like the soldiers to "New France" or religious fraternities like the Barr Colonists who settled in Alberta.

Many, in the West, were deliberately recruited, drawn from Europe by promises of land and freedom.

Others sought sanctuary from persecution or turmoil at home – I remember the small hotels, along Ninth Avenue in Calgary, packed, in 1956, with Hungarians who had fled here after their revolution was repressed. Hundreds of thousands of Canadians trace their origins to similar flights, from Nazi regimes, or Soviet, or from oppression in Asia or Africa or the Americas.

But, most often, those decisions were personal and practical, driven by a desire to find opportunities that were impossible at home. So, if there was no single story, there was a common pattern to the thinking that settled Canada.

My own family kept few records, but what I know suggests

they came to a new country because they could not stay at home. My mother's mother was sent from Galway, in her early teens, to Boston, to keep house for an aunt whom she had never met, because there was no money and no work in Ireland. She was welcomed, in the new world, by signs advising "No Irish need apply," and so had no alternative to her aunt, until she married.

A generation earlier, my father's grandfather could not make a living in his native Tiree, and came to farm in Ontario, settling finally in Bruce County, near Kincardine.

My ancestors may have had some sense of what they were coming to, but I suspect their real motive was simply to leave where they couldn't stay.

In time, those families became active in their communities, and churches, and country. But I doubt they came with much sense of building a nation. Their purpose would have been more personal – to earn a living, to start and keep a family, to make themselves secure.

And that has been the story of most Canadians. They came for personal reasons, and built their new lives and communities quietly and gradually, without much sense of larger mission.

(There are, of course, some grander souls, who trace their ancestry back to famous names and old regimes – I remember once, in the late 1960s, fresh from High River, making conversation at a reception in Ottawa, and asking someone whose name I had not quite caught whether he had ever been to Louisiana. "Been there?" he sniffed. "My family discovered it." Perhaps he was a Métis. But there is not much of that ancestral hubris in Canada.)

Most Canadians came to their new country to improve their own lives, and they built their society pragmatically, as they went.

That stands in contrast to the stated purpose south of the

forty-ninth parallel, in this new continent. The United States set out to change history, and self-consciously create a "new society." That sense of purpose and identity is an integral part of the national character of the United States, for better and for worse. And we Canadians are different.

Perhaps, had our own history been more messianic, there would be a compelling pan-Canadian sense of identity, a reaching for the heart when the anthem played, that would have protected us against drift or separation. But that isn't what happened. We developed less dramatically, less ideologically. And, step by pragmatic step, we built the community which today is judged the "best place in the world to live."

That is the second element of Canada to consider — what we are today, and how that community compares to other societies, which have natural assets similar to ours, but have developed them in different ways.

Let me return to a familiar theme. What is admired about Canada is not simply our undoubted wealth and beauty, attributes which many countries share, but the kind of society we have built with those resources. Some of the qualities that distinguish Canada — our medicare and pension program, our instinct to respect others and to seek agreement — do not grow naturally in North America. They are a distinctive product of Canada.

Internationally, what is respected about Canada is not simply our high ideals, which many other communities espouse, but how we apply those ideals in actual practice — how we perform.

Internationally, what causes other nations to turn to Canada when there are tensions to defuse, or differences to bridge, is that we prove ourselves to be consistently even-handed and pragmatic, and often successful.

We are, of course, a democratic society with a strong and

serious commitment to human rights and human freedom, in Canada and abroad. We are a market economy, convinced of the global importance of freer trade and bringing down our own barriers. Those are essential characteristics of the Canada that the world admires.

But our unique reputation is based on more than that. Canada is a country judged by results. And this is an age in which results matter much more than they used to.

There is a debate about whether or not "ideology is dead." The debate itself is instructive because, not long ago, economies in Eastern Europe were hamstrung by Marxist models, and intellectuals in the United States were hauled before a Committee on UnAmerican Activities. It is worth reflecting that refugees from both "isms" – Marx and McCarthy – came to Canada, and made their way in our tolerant and undemonstrative community.

In my view, the secret of Canada's success is that this is a very pragmatic country. Although our political philosophers range across the spectrum, and political parties like the CCF/NDP have struggled to build a national base, our public policy has not been based on philosophic differences, as in Europe or, increasingly, the United States.

We have clear values, about which we can be copiously preachy, and our record at respecting what we say we believe is more consistent than that of most nations. But our standard is to judge problems on their merits, not as tests of principle, and then solve them.

Our domestic public policy – from Sir John's railway to medicare, to proposals for child care – has aimed at practical results, not philosophical victories. We established crown corporations, and a mixed economy, because we had too much geography for common services to be profitable. We established our social security system because we have too many extremes of climate and resources for citizens to cope on their own.

The most interesting question about Canada is: what might we become if we could harness and focus all the creative energies which are pulling Canadians in different directions today? This country is full of initiative and optimism and pride. I find it everywhere – in Halifax, in Chicoutimi, among new Canadians, among aboriginal leaders, everywhere. Ironically, those qualities are also pronounced among the influential citizens who fight in the trenches of this long-distance war that is debilitating Canada. Many of the activist citizens who voted Reform in the West, and support separatism in Quebec, share a common energy and optimism. They are convincing themselves they are enemies, yet, usually, they have never met; moreover, in my judgement, if they would come together they would find a lot of common cause. I am not speaking here of the leaders of those movements, who might prove to be harder cases, with agendas of their own, but of the activists, the people rooted so deeply in their own communities that they have not had an opportunity to come to know the Canadians they are straining against.

What a waste it is to have these energies pulling against one another. Not only does that threaten the future integrity of Canada, but it exacts a high cost today, simply because talents that should be creating jobs or opportunities in Montreal or Halifax or Edmonton are diverted to a struggle against other Canadians. Think of how strong a country we could be – with Canada's location, and trade agreements, and social structure, and natural wealth – if Canadians in Calgary and Quebec City and Toronto and Inuvik would pull deliberately together.

This is an unusal time in the world. Naked power matters less than it used to, and skill and example matter more. That is obviously true in international affairs, where the capacity to make peace is suddenly more important than the threat to make war. As a former foreign minister, I know that the conciliatory, pragmatic talents of Canada have never been more needed, by a troubled world, than they are today. There has never before been a period when the qualities that characterize Canada fit the world so well. This is Canada's time.

It is also Canada's time at home. Our differences of language and geography and perception are a world apart from the forces that tear at truly divided societies. Moreover, they are precisely the kinds of differences that Canadians, on our record, are better able to resolve than almost any other people. If we have the will.

Even with our heavy debt, our economy is naturally strong, and has become much more competitive in critical international markets. Inherently, the Canadian economy is among the strongest in the world; again, the only real issue is whether we have the will to bring out that strength.

Compared with any other country, our society is healthy. We are, of course, vulnerable to drugs and violence and greed, and the other cancers of the modern world, but our social structure is sound and inclusive. Apart from some aboriginal communities, and some homeless Canadians, very few of our citizens are marginalized or excluded, as in other rich societies. Specific social programs will change, of course, but the principle is solidly established that the Canadian community will care for citizens in need. The respect for equality runs deep in our society, and is now reinforced by the Charter of Rights and Freedoms.

None of that is a guarantee that Canada will succeed. Indeed, despite all our advantages, we are closer to coming apart, as a national community, than we have ever been before. Our choice is simple: to drift into smaller parts, or to become, finally, a nation as large as our geography and our potential. If we choose a large Canada, we can become one of the handful of nations which, in the next decades, will define the values and the nature of the modern world. That future depends on each of us. If our citizens want to make the most of this remarkable country, now is the time.